Israel Becomes a Nation

Clare Amos, M.A.
Lecturer in Old Testament Studies at Westcott House, Cambridge

Advisory Editor
The Reverend John Pridmore
Head of Religious Studies
King Edward's School, Witley

Hulton Educational

Introduction

Israel Becomes a Nation introduces the reader to the world of the Hebrew Scriptures down to and including the time of David and Solomon. The book is written with the conviction that the events related by the Scriptures cannot be studied in isolation. They only make sense when viewed against the backcloth provided by the geography of the Middle East and the history and culture of the various peoples with whom the Israelites became involved as they progressed towards becoming a nation. Among the subjects treated in this book, therefore, is the geography of the land of Canaan and the religion of the Canaanite peoples whom the Israelites encountered there. These are not 'optional extras' but an integral part of the story.

This book deals with a period of history in which oral tradition was much more important than written sources. For this reason the question of who wrote the individual biblical books has not been considered in great detail, with the exception of the writer/editor responsible for the J strand of the Pentateuch which is generally agreed to come from the time of David and Solomon. The first section of this book sets the scene at the time when the history of the people was first recorded in written form. It presents the idea that history is always coloured by the 'spectacles'—the values, ideas and beliefs—of the people who recount it.

It is assumed throughout *Israel Becomes a Nation* that there is no adequate substitute for the text of the Bible itself. Students should therefore read the appropriate passages set in each section before turning to this book. The text normally used here is that of the *Good News Bible* (The Bible Societies/Collins/Fontana), although from time to time reference is made to the *Revised Standard Version*, particularly for discussion of well-known theological terms (e.g., the *RSV*'s 'Feast of Booths' has been preferred to the *GN*'s 'Feast of Shelters').

Israel Becomes a Nation is the first book in the series *Discovering the Bible*. Like the others, it is designed for use up to 'O' level standard, but it is hoped that the format will make it available to a wide range of ability or interest, including CSE and non-examination groups.

Each spread is designed as a single unit and may be used as the basis for a single lesson. Each section consists of two or three spreads, and in addition background material and critical issues are dealt with in boxes, which could be omitted by less advanced students. Thus the topics may be studied at a number of different levels.

CA

Other titles in the series Discovering the Bible are:
The Progress of God's People
Jesus and the Gospels
The Expansion of Christianity

Acknowledgements

The author and publishers thank the following for permission to reproduce copyright photographs on these pages:

J. Allan Cash, 12, 28, 32, 48
Council of Christians and Jews, 7, 33, 49, 58
Robert Harding Picture Library, 22
Sonia Halliday Photographs, 15, 17, 27, 35, 38, 41, 43, 46 (bottom), 50, 54 (right), 59, 62, 66, 67, 70–71, 78, 81 (left), 85, 86
Mansell Collection, 31, 37, 52, 60, 72, 73
Photoresources, 46 (top), 57
Ronald Sheridan Photo-Library, 6, 8, 10, 11, 21, 23, 25, 29, 36, 53 (left), 65, 74, 80
Jamie Simson, 81 (right)
Woodmansterne Ltd, 71

Artwork by Anna Hancock
Maps and diagrams by Roy Jones
Edited and designed by Ela Ginalska

First published in Great Britain 1984 by
Hulton Educational Publications Ltd, Raans Road,
Amersham, Bucks HP6 6JJ

Text © Clare Amos 1984
Illustrations © Hulton Educational 1984

ISBN 0 7175 1160 X

Phototypeset by Input Typesetting Ltd, London
Printed in Great Britain by Fletcher & Son Ltd.,
Norwich. Bound by Richard Clay (The Chaucer Press)
Ltd., Bungay, Suffolk

Contents

1 Beginning at the end

A united kingdom

The time is about 975 BC; the place—Jerusalem. King David, or perhaps his son Solomon, sits on the throne. The twelve tribes of Israel are more or less united under the king, although there are rumblings, which will grow louder as the years pass, about the 'favouritism' shown to people from the tribe of Judah, the tribe to which David and Solomon themselves belong. However, it is not just over 'Israelites' that David and Solomon now rule—not just over those people whose ancestors escaped from Egypt and entered the land of Canaan three centuries or so ago. For the kingdom of David and Solomon includes many people whom we could best describe as native 'Canaanites', whose ancestors have lived in the land of Canaan for centuries, as far back as anyone can remember.

Originally the Israelites were wandering shepherds in the ancient Middle East, with herds of sheep and goats.

The Canaanites

These people lived in walled cities, or in villages grouped around cities, so that they could take refuge inside these walls whenever danger threatened. Most of them were farmers, supporting themselves by growing wheat and barley, and cultivating olives, figs and vines, for that was the traditional way of life in the land of Canaan [Deuteronomy 8:7–8]. Some of the Canaanites, though, were merchants or traders, since Canaan stood at the crossroads of the ancient Middle East. For the last few hundred years the Canaanites had known a much higher standard of living and culture than the Israelites, for they had had the leisure which settled people have to develop the skills of working metals, making beautiful pottery, creating musical instruments and musical skills, and above all using the art of writing.

Farming the land is still a difficult job in the hilly country that was once called Canaan.

The Israelites

The Israelites, on the other hand, had previously been nomads—shepherds wandering in the wilderness, beyond the borders of the land where the Canaanites were settled. There wasn't enough water there to grow cereal crops, and so they scratched a living by keeping goats, some sheep and donkeys, and searching out pasture for their animals. And as the pasture in one area was used up, they would need to move on, probably to an oasis, where a natural spring in the desert would be surrounded by a patch of green, contrasting with the stark barrenness of the land around.

It was a difficult life the Israelites had had, and one that did not allow for any luxuries. And although the Israelites had crossed the Jordan and entered the land of Canaan a long time ago, they had still to continue in a largely nomadic existence, for they had not been strong enough to conquer many of the fortified Canaanite cities. They had had to avoid the fertile lowlands where the Canaanites were powerful and where their war chariots could be used. Thus the Israelites continued to live an unsettled life on the heights of the rocky hills.

It is quite likely that the high ziggurats of Mesopotamia were in the biblical writer's mind when he told the story of the Tower of Babel (Genesis 11:1–9).

Cain and Abel

Read Genesis 4:1–5

One of the stories that the Israelites would have often told is the account of the quarrel between Cain and Abel. Like many Old Testament stories it has several layers, and can speak to us in a variety of ways. However, one of the meanings of the tale of Cain's murder of his brother Abel is to point out that there is often hostility and enmity between people who follow different ways of life. Abel is a shepherd, personifying the nomadic way of life, while Cain is a farmer growing crops from the soil. It is interesting to see how in this story it is Abel—the nomad—who is pictured in a favourable light, while Cain, the farmer, is the villain of the piece. Perhaps this is partly because the story is told from the perspective of the Israelites, who were originally nomads, and it therefore tells us something of the nomads' distrust of those, like the

Canaanites, who led a very different life.

In several places in the Hebrew Scriptures we can sense a similar distrust of people who lived a settled life as farmers or in cities. For the Scriptures recognised that, though a settled life provides many opportunities, there are also dangers attached. After the flood, Noah tills the ground and becomes a farmer. Eventually, however, this leads to his getting extremely drunk [Genesis 9:20–23]. It is those who live in a city who try to build a tower up to heaven and refuse to take any account of God [Genesis 11:1–9].

The Israelites were not the only people who told stories about the tensions and competition between shepherds and farmers. There is a story from Mesopotamia in which a shepherd and a farmer both compete to win the love of a beautiful goddess. In this story the farmer eventually wins—perhaps this is because the story was told by people who were themselves farmers.

5

David and Jerusalem

With the coming of David, the Israelites' un-settled position changed. David's charismatic personality, his skills as a leader in war, and perhaps also his political acumen, meant that the Israelites could now conquer peoples and cities that had previously been too strong for them. The climax was the capture of Jerusalem, which David took by a very clever stratagem (see section 16). It was one of the great moments of Israelite history and left its impact on the whole of the Hebrew Scriptures: from the time of David, Jerusalem becomes 'the Holy City', the focus of the nation's desire and longing [see **Psalm 122**].

However, like all great moments in history, the capture of Jerusalem provided both *challenges* and *opportunities*. It called for many decisions to be made. What was to happen to the Canaanites who had lived in the city before its capture by David? Were they to be killed in large numbers, as often happened in ancient warfare? We are fairly sure that this did not happen after David's capture of Jerusalem. Instead, the inhabitants of Jerusalem—and probably also other Canaanite cities captured by David—were 'assimilated': they joined with the Israelites to become part of David and Solomon's kingdom.

Problems and dangers

This meant the Canaanites were in a position to influence the Israelites greatly. Was this influence to be for good, or for bad? Undoubtedly the Israelites had much to learn from the Canaanites about the material aspects of civilisation—and this was good. They also wanted to learn much from them about agriculture, because now the Israelites themselves were in a position to end their previous nomadic lifestyle, to settle down and become farmers, to produce 'grain, wine and oil' [**Hosea 2:8**].

However, there was also a problem—the Canaanites worshipped gods who were different from the God worshipped by the Israelites. Their gods were closely connected with agriculture and the growing of crops. We can imagine the Canaanites saying to the Israelites, 'Why not worship our gods? After all, they

A figurine of the goddess Astarte holding a bird. The Canaanites worshipped several deities, notably Baal (see page 46), whose wife and sister was Anat, and El, king of the gods, who was married to Asherah.

belong to this country, and they are concerned with the way we live here. Your God—he's is a god of the desert, of the wilderness, what use is he here in this land of Canaan?' The Hebrew Scriptures make it very clear that this was a big problem, a problem that began in the time of the Judges, but surely became much more critical in the time of David, when his military successes meant that Israelites and Canaanites were brought so close together. We know a great deal about the gods of the Canaanites (see section 11) and can see how closely they were bound up with farming and growing crops, which was the way the Canaanites lived. So when the Israelites themselves became farmers, it must have seemed the 'sensible' thing to many of them to change their gods as they changed their way of life. The fact that not all the Israelites did so, and many remained loyal to the God their ancestors had worshipped in the desert, the God who had brought them out of Egypt, is surely a sign that the God whom the Israelites had met in Egypt and in the desert

The Jewish people continue to attach great importance to their history—only now it is written down, not oral. They pay great respect to the scrolls of the Law, or 'Torah'. Here a boy reads from the 'Torah' in a synagogue.

was real to them.

There were other dangers and problems to be faced as well, for the military and political successes of David and Solomon raised questions. They meant that Israel could now take its place on the stage of the Middle East; it could now be a nation 'like all the nations' [Deuteronomy 17:14]. However, Israel had originally not been a nation at all, but a religious community, a group of people whose common bond was not political but religious, who were common worshippers of the God who had brought them out of Egypt. If Israel became a nation like other nations, could it truly remain Israel? That was a tension and a question which continued for many centuries.

The first scriptures

So much for the dangers. But the time of David was a time of great opportunity too. One of the most important things that happened was the beginning of Israelite literature, the literature that eventually became the Hebrew Scriptures. For now the Israelites were able to write down their history, their sacred history, the account of the ways God had helped and guided their ancestors. It is doubtful if writing was much used by the Israelites before the time of David—nomadic people find it difficult to carry written texts around with them! Instead they learn their history orally, by word of mouth, the elders of the tribe teaching the young people. This still happens among the nomadic peoples of the Middle East. This method of preserving history is known as *oral tradition*, and frequently it is very accurate. People who do not have access to books and computers often have very good memories because they need them! But in the time of David it became possible for the Israelites to record their history fully in writing. As they did so, they tried to work out what had been God's purpose in bringing them to the land of Canaan and guiding them to the political success they had now experienced under David.

One of the most important reasons for recording their history was to retell it when they worshipped God. They thanked God for the gracious way he had treated them and their ancestors. They remembered with gratitude how he had brought them out of the land of Egypt and into the land of Canaan. But they would go even further back in history than that, and recall how God had brought their ancestors from far away, from Mesopotamia. So to record their history was necessary for the Israelites—for how else could they adequately worship God, who was the Lord of their history? In the Book of Deuteronomy we can see clearly just what would have happened. During the Israelite 'harvest festival' the Israelite worshipper goes to the temple to offer to God the first fruits of his crops. As he does so he remembers God's blessings to the Israelite people, not just in the bounty of the harvest, but also his gracious acts in history. And so the worshipper offers thanks beginning with the words, 'A wandering Aramaean was my father . . .' [Deuteronomy 26:5–11].

2 Abraham, the wandering Aramaean

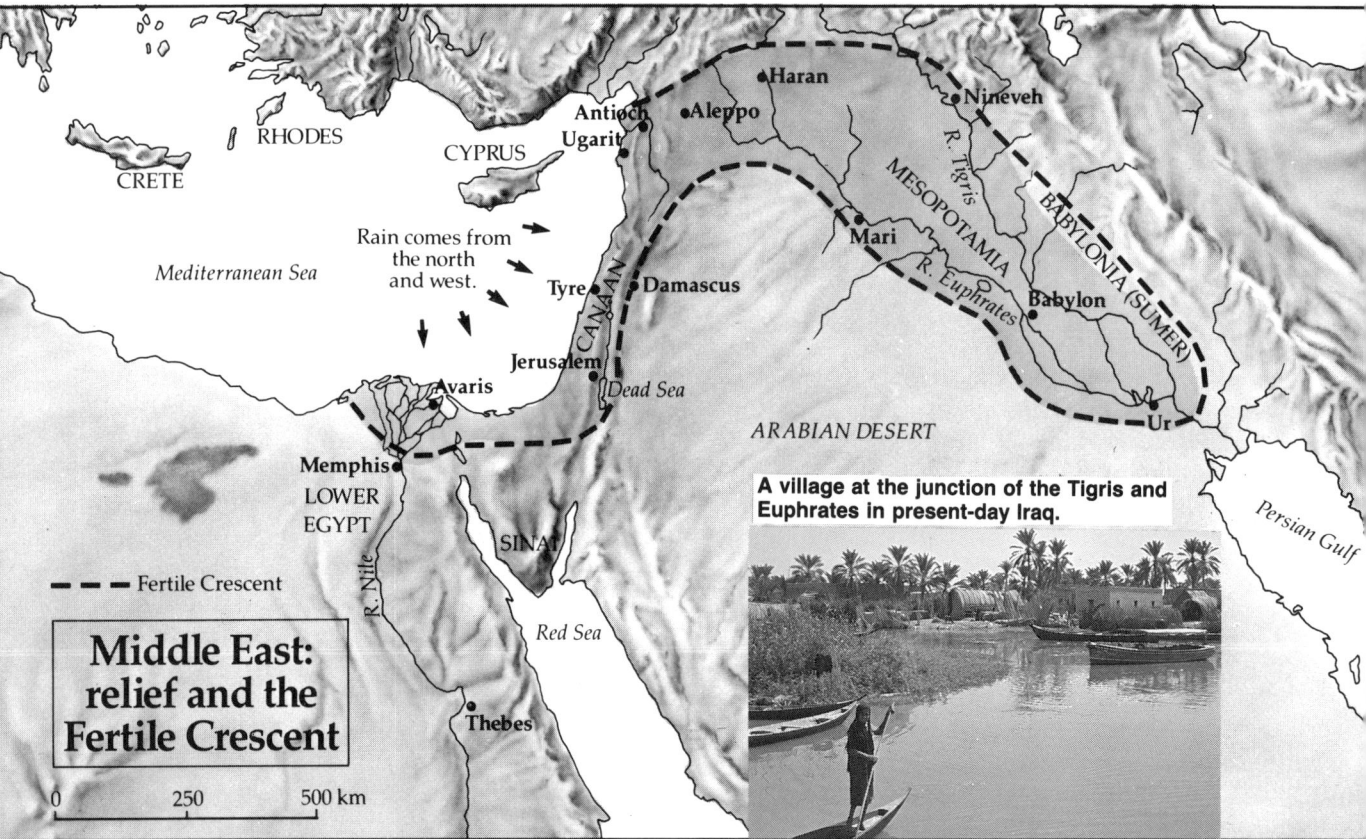

Rain comes from the north and west.

Mediterranean Sea

RHODES
CRETE
CYPRUS

Haran
Antioch •Aleppo •Nineveh
Ugarit
MESOPOTAMIA
R. Tigris
Mari
BABYLONIA (SUMER)
Tyre• Damascus
R. Euphrates
Babylon
CANAAN
Jerusalem•
Dead Sea
Avaris
ARABIAN DESERT
Ur
Memphis•
LOWER EGYPT
SINAI
Persian Gulf
R. Nile
Red Sea
Thebes

– – – Fertile Crescent

Middle East: relief and the Fertile Crescent

0   250   500 km

A village at the junction of the Tigris and Euphrates in present-day Iraq.

When the Israelites remembered what God had done for them and their ancestors, they would begin by recalling how he had brought Abraham from Mesopotamia to the land of Canaan. To understand just what that involved, we need to take a look at the map of the Middle East.

The Fertile Crescent

A people's history is always affected by the geography of the land where they live. In fact, geography is *especially* important when we try to understand the history of the Middle East. This is partly because there are so many geographical extremes close together in one region: you move very quickly from luxuriant green to barren desert.

Look carefully at the map on this page. It distinguishes between areas that are desert and those that are fertile. You can see that the great majority of the Middle East is desert—it receives too little rain to grow anything. Geographers define a desert as being an area receiving less than 100mm of rain each year. This is the case with much of the Middle East. Rainfall is, of course, brought by clouds which travel in from the sea—but in the Middle East the only sizeable sea is the Mediterranean. Rainclouds do travel eastwards coming from the Mediterranean Sea, but they quickly drop their moisture over the lands nearest to the coast. So, as you can see clearly from the map, the land of Canaan itself is quite fertile, because it is 'a land watered by rain' **[Deuteronomy 11:11]**. However, by the time the clouds reach east of Jerusalem or Damascus they have dropped most of their moisture, so there is very little left for the areas further east!

Look again at the map. There is an area a long way to the east that is indicated as being fertile. That is the region we have already referred to as *Mesopotamia*, a word that means 'between the rivers'. Mesopotamia is the area of land that lies between the Tigris and the Euphrates. It is these rivers which make the area fertile. They rise in the high mountains of Turkey and each year bring down flood waters from the melting snows of the Turkish mountains. Now, if you look at the areas shown as fertile on the map, you will notice that they form a kind of semicircle. For this reason these fertile areas of the Middle East are usually referred to as 'the Fertile Crescent'. In the Middle East it is only within the Fertile Crescent that it is possible to live the settled life of a farmer; outside the Fertile Crescent farming is not possible.

Abraham's journey

Read Genesis 11:31–32, 12
The Book of Genesis tells us that Abraham travelled with his father Terah from Ur of the Chaldeans to Haran in north Mesopotamia. Then, after Terah's death, he was called by God to uproot himself again and move on to the land of Canaan. If you look at the map, you can see this means that Abraham would have had to travel round the edges of the Fertile Crescent as he journeyed from Ur, north to Haran, and then south-west to Canaan. It would have been very difficult, perhaps impossible, for anyone to travel directly west from Ur to Canaan, since this would have involved a very long journey across extremely arid desert. Even nomadic peoples preferred to stay as close as possible to the fringes of the fertile land. Today, Arab nomads do make long journeys through arid desert, but they can do this because they use camels much more than Abraham and his contemporaries did. In Abraham's time, nomadic people used donkeys rather more than camels as their pack animals. Donkeys need to be watered much more often than camels. This meant that the nomads of Abraham's day were much more restricted in their movements than are modern desert-dwellers.

When and why did Abraham and Terah make the long journey from Ur? Most scholars would suggest that Abraham's journey took place sometime between 1800 and 1700 BC. It was a long, slow journey that lasted beyond Terah's lifetime. Probably we should imagine the family travelling in a large, plodding caravan, including all their 'kin', their servants and their animals. Abraham and Terah were not the only group of people who were travelling from east to west round the Fertile Crescent at that time. For the beginning of the second millenium BC was a period of great disturbances in the Middle East. The brilliant civilisation of the Sumerians, which had flourished in southern Mesopotamia based on Ur for most of the third millenium BC, was suddenly overthrown in 1950 BC. A power vacuum then developed in the area, and this gave an opportunity for a group of nomadic people to push northwards from the deserts of the Arabian Peninsula up into Mesopotamia.

The Amorites

Unlike the Sumerians, the nomads who invaded Mesopotamia were a *Semitic* people (descendants of Shem), and their language was a semitic language related to Hebrew. They were known as *Amorites*. As they grew stronger, they pushed their way further and further north, eventually managing to move into the fertile land and establishing their capital at the city of Mari in northern Mesopotamia. These nomadic Amorites were greatly feared by those who lived settled lives in the great cities of Mesopotamia, such as Mari. There is a text which comes from Mari that jibes at the Amorites, 'The Amorites who know not houses, who know not towns, uncouth mountain dwellers.' The sophisticated people of the Mesopotamian cities despised the Amorites for their wildness. On the other hand, it was through their wildness and ferocity that the Amorites were eventually able to seize power in cities like Mari.

The journey that Terah and Abraham made from Ur to Haran might well be related to the movement of populations that accompanied the Amorite invasion. At one point, in fact, the Hebrew Scriptures specifically describe Israel's ancestors as being Amorites: 'Your father was an Amorite' [Ezekiel 17:3].

Abraham the Hebrew

Another term which is used to describe Abraham is 'Hebrew' [**Genesis 14:13**]. Now, the biblical word Hebrew probably means the same as the word Habiru which is found in many Mesopotamian texts that are roughly contemporary with Abraham. In these texts the term Habiru is used to describe people who were 'outsiders', people on the fringes of society. Because they were not really fully accepted by the 'insiders', these Habiru had to live as best they could, sometimes hiring themselves out as mercenary soldiers, sometimes selling themselves as slave labourers, sometimes being no more than rather disreputable nomads and wanderers.

As they journey round the fertile crescent, Terah and Abraham fit into this picture. They did not settle down and become part of any of the cities of Mesopotamia and, even when he eventually reaches the land of Canaan, Abraham is still described as a 'sojourner', one not permanently integrated into the society of Canaan. And in Genesis 14 we can observe Abraham 'the Hebrew' fighting other people's battles as a mercenary soldier in a similar way to that in which the Mesopotamian texts describe the Habiru soldiers.

So, when the Old Testament describes Abraham as a 'Hebrew', we are probably meant to picture him as a wanderer somewhat outside the fringes of settled society in the ancient Middle East. As we shall see, at a later time Abraham's descendants were also called Hebrews, and at this time the term also seems to refer to a rather inferior status. A third name that the Old Testament uses to describe Abraham is 'Aramaean' [**Deuteronomy 26:5**]. Aramaean probably means something similar to Amorite, and this was the way in which later generations often referred to the Amorites.

Family names and customs

There are two ways we can find out more about the way Abraham and his family lived. We can look at tablets that have been discovered in archaeological excavations of the great cities of the ancient Middle East. We can also study the way of life of Arab nomads of the recent past and modern times.

We have already seen how texts from Mari throw light on the times of Abraham and the Amorites. Many of the Mari texts contain names very similar to biblical names. For instance, the Mari texts refer to somebody called Jacob-El, which reminds us of the biblical Jacob, Abraham's grandson, and the same texts also speak of a group of people called the Benjaminites, whose name is identical with that of the tribe of Benjamin. It is unlikely that the Mari texts are here talking of precisely the same people who appear in the Bible, but the similarity of names is still important, for it seems to show that the names given to Abraham and his family were common names at this particular time in the ancient Middle East.

There are other ancient cities where interesting tablets have been found which seem to shed light on the social customs practised by Abraham and his family. Particularly important are tablets from Babylon and Nuzu. Babylon was a city of major significance during this period, and its king, Hammurabi, wrote a lawcode that had great influence in the region. One of the laws of Hammurabi concerns the situation which can arise when a wife is barren and unable to bear children for her husband. Hammurabi states that if this happens she may give

Cuneiform text on a clay tablet found by archaeologists in Mesopotamia.

Hammurabi's lawcode, engraved on this stele, affected much of the ancient world.

something that happens in the life of Abraham. Sarah, Abraham's wife, is apparently unable to have any children, so she gives Abraham Hagar, her maidservant. Hagar bears a son, Ishmael, for Abraham. This seems to fit in very well with the laws of Hammurabi. But then when Sarah does miraculously have a son, Isaac, in her old age, she resents Hagar's and Ishmael's position and tries to get them sent away. Abraham, however, remembering the laws of the time, does not really want to allow this to happen. In the end, though, he agrees **[Genesis 16:1–16, 21:8–14]**.

Some customs from the city of Nuzu, a city which was situated to the east of the Tigris river, also seem to appear in the biblical stories of Abraham and Sarah. Twice we hear that Abraham pretends that Sarah was his sister rather than his wife. The reason for this seems to be that Sarah was very beautiful, and Abraham believed that if people knew she was his wife they would kill him and seize her. All the same, to pretend that your wife is your sister appears a strange thing to do! However, we can read on the tablets discovered at Nuzu that it was common for men to 'adopt' their wives and regard them as sisters as well as wives. Perhaps the story of Abraham and Sarah reflects this custom **[Genesis 12:10–20, 20:1–18]**.

her husband her maid-servant to be his slave-wife and to have children on her behalf. But then the law-code is quite clear—if a slave-wife does bear children, then she must not be sold or dismissed. This law helps to make sense of

The wedge-writing of Mesopotamia

The art of writing was extremely important to the people of Mesopotamia. Their culture depended upon it. Only through written records could the kings of the great cities know who and where had paid their taxes; only so could they record the complicated laws, customs and alliances which helped to maintain the peace in the land of the Two Rivers.

Writing, though, was a complicated business in Babylon and Mari. First you took a lump of clay—easy to find in the flood plains of the rivers. Then, using a wedge-shaped stylus, you cut a series of marks into the still-damp clay. This process gave the writing its name 'cuneiform' or 'wedge-writing'. Finally, you had to bake the clay hard in a hot oven. Once this was done the writing became permanent—so

permanent that archaeologists coming upon written clay tablets many centuries later might have thought they were baked yesterday.

Why was this process so complicated? The problem was knowing which combination of wedges to use to make the symbol you wanted. Mesopotamian writing was *syllabic*, not *alphabetic*. This means that each symbol in Mesopotamian writing was equal to an English syllable, not to a single letter. There was a symbol for *sa*, a different one for *si*, another for *so*, others again for *san* or *sun*. Start counting! You can see that the possible permutations are enormous. The number of different symbols in Mesopotamian writing ran into several thousands. So this meant to learn how to write in ancient Mesopotamia was a skill that took many years to learn. Only a few specialists would do so. Ordinary people would never think of learning to read or write.

The nomad way of life

Beduin nomads encamped on the road to the Dead Sea. Their way of life has not changed much since the time of Abraham.

To know more about the day-to-day life of Abraham we can also look at the way in which Arab nomads live in the Middle East today. The common term for these modern nomads is 'Beduin'. Their lifestyle has not altered significantly during the last 4000 years. Only in very recent times have modern inventions such as cars, radio and television begun to make some impact on their way of life.

We can imagine Abraham living in a black tent made out of goats' hair. Other members of Abraham's caravan, his relative Lot and his servant Eliezer, would have set up similar tents nearby. Each tent would be divided into two. There would be one section reserved for the women, and the other part would be for the men and would be where visitors were entertained. Abraham and Sarah would have dressed in similar fashion to the Beduin of today—very important would be the head-dress worn by both men and women as protection against the burning sun of the desert. Their food would

consist of what they could provide for themselves: milk from sheep and goats, soured milk similar to modern yogurt, and on special occasions an animal would be killed and eaten. Sometimes it would be possible to grow a little barley near the tents and this would have been ground and baked into flat, unleavened barley bread.

Tribes and clans

The way society was organised at the time of Abraham was quite different to the way it is organised in industrialised countries today. For us, society is structured on the basis of *place*. We see ourselves as citizens of a particular country, e.g. the United Kingdom, and further define ourselves as living in a particular county and perhaps town. But this is impossible if you are a nomad. It makes no sense at all to describe yourself as an inhabitant of a particular country or city, since you don't intend to stay there for very long. So society among modern

12

To nomads, the stories that tell the history of their tribe are important. The old men pass them on to the youngsters.

might perhaps be chosen as 'chieftain'. But this was only a temporary arrangement and, when the danger was past, the chieftain reverted to being an ordinary member of the tribe once again. In such a family-based society it was important to know precisely who you were, so genealogies were very significant. As members of the family or clan gathered round the camp fire in the evening, the old men of the group would teach the youngsters the family traditions—how it was that the family and tribe had moved to this region, why it was that they were friendly with the tribe who lived to the east of them but waged a continual war with the tribes who lived to the north. So, for example, at a later time the tribes of Israel were to learn that the Israelites were closely related to the Edomites, because their common ancestors Jacob and Esau had been brothers. On the other hand, the reason they spent a great deal of time fighting the Edomites was because Jacob and Esau had quarrelled. Family genealogy explained tribal history. We shall see that the tribal way of life remained important for Abraham's descendants for a very long time, until they were firmly settled in the land of Canaan.

Beduin—and among ancient nomads like Abraham—is organised on the basis of *family* or *kinship*. When we speak of a family in this context, we do not mean our modern 'nuclear family' of father, mother and two children, but rather an 'extended family' including several generations and quite distant cousins. Several 'families' who were related to each other would have made up a 'clan', and several 'clans' went to make up a 'tribe'. Members of the same family, clan and tribe all had very definite obligations towards each other. They had to help one another whenever danger or trouble threatened. They even had the duty of fighting to 'avenge' a member of the tribe who had been killed.

In this family-based way of life, all the men were treated equally. There was no place for kings or absolute rulers. All the male members of the family or tribe had a voice in decisions, although the old men or 'elders' were usually listened to with particular respect. Whenever the tribe had to fight in battle, one individual

Ebla—a forgotten civilisation

Archaeology does not stand still. Archaeologists are always on the lookout for new cities to explore, new civilisations to discover. One recent discovery that has thrilled the archaeological world has been the finding of Ebla, the remains of a great city which once dominated the lands to the west of Mesopotamia. Excavations started at Ebla in the early 1960s. There were several years in which very little was found. But then in 1975 the archaeologists' patience was rewarded— a vast number of cuneiform tablets were found which told the history of Ebla and gave an inkling of how great an empire it had once ruled.

Ebla flourished around 2500 BC—some centuries before the lifetime of Abraham. All the same, as the Ebla tablets are deciphered in the coming years, they are likely to shed new light on the turbulent world of the ancient Middle East into which Abraham was born.

3 Abraham, man of faith and promise

Whatever political or social factors may have been involved in Abraham's journey from Ur to Haran and then round to the land of Canaan, as far as the Old Testament is concerned it was also a journey made at God's direct command. There is no contradiction here. The faith of the Bible is that God can work through and use human politics and history to bring about his ultimate purposes.

Abraham's God

What was Abraham's understanding of the God who called him in faith to leave his father's house and travel into the unknown? Most probably Abraham thought of God as an invisible member of the family or tribe. Generally, the way in which people think about God is deeply influenced by their own experiences. Because concepts such as family and kinship were so important to Abraham, it was in 'family' terms that he understood and thought about God. So did Isaac and Jacob somewhat later on. The later Israelites grouped Abraham, Isaac and Jacob together and referred to them as the 'patriarchs'. This is a word that means 'ancestors'. The Hebrew Scriptures give us some of the titles by which the patriarchs referred to God. These include 'Shield of Abraham' [**Genesis 15:1**], 'Kinsman of Isaac' [**Genesis 31:42**] and 'Mighty One of Jacob' [**Genesis 49:24**]. Such titles do indeed make it clear that the patriarchs thought of God as an invisible member of the extended family—calling God 'Kinsman of Isaac' makes this quite apparent. However, these titles also show that the patriarchs believed God to be essentially their protector. We can well understand why. The desert was a frightening place: there were wild animals and hostile tribes to be encountered—life was very uncertain. One needed a God to help and protect in all the dangers that could be met. To call God 'Shield of Abraham' or 'Mighty One of Jacob' was to say precisely that.

This protector God was also necessarily a God who could travel with his people. One of the characteristics of nomadic religion, of the religion of people like Abraham, was believing that God could move about with them. After all, he would not be much use if he had to be left behind at the last oasis! The religion of settled farmers like the Canaanites was very different. They believed that the gods lived in a temple and were rooted to one particular spot. If you wanted to approach the gods, you had to visit the temple. Abraham's understanding of God was not like this at all. For him, God was not confined to one particular spot, but was able to move around with all his people, guiding them and protecting them. We can say that this is the very heart and essence of the Biblical idea of the nature of God.

Abraham's only son

Read Genesis 22

Abraham is not only important because of the way in which he understood God, but also because of the way in which he responded to him. God called Abraham to set out on a journey to a completely unknown land, with many likely dangers to be encountered on the way. All God promised was that he would be with Abraham. And Abraham believed and trusted and followed where God was leading him. Right up to the New Testament Abraham is therefore considered the supreme example of faith. 'It is the men of faith who are sons of Abraham . . . those who are men of faith are blessed along with Abraham who had faith.' [**Galatians 3:7–9**]. We could find several other examples in the New Testament. What we can say therefore is that with Abraham the note of faith, of trust in God's promises and in his ability to fulfil them, appears in the Bible—and after Abraham we could really describe the whole Bible as the story of a people travelling in pilgrimage in response to God's summons and leading.

Abraham's faith was to be tested in a very real way. The birth of Isaac, his son, had been a miracle, for both Abraham and Sarah were far too old to have any children. Isaac therefore was doubly precious to Abraham. However, while Isaac was growing up, perhaps when he was about twelve years old, Abraham began to feel that God was asking him to sacrifice his son. Human sacrifice is a custom that sounds very strange to us, but we should remember that in the Ancient Middle East many of the neighbours of the Israelites did sacrifice their first-born children to their gods. They might do so in times of particular danger and stress. So, for example, Mesha King of Moab sacrificed his son when he was besieged by the Israelites [**II Kings 3:27**]. Therefore Abraham, looking at the way his neighbours were willing to sacrifice their children to their gods, may have felt that his commitment to his God demanded that he should make the supreme sacrifice of his beloved son Isaac. The Hebrew Scriptures make it quite clear that God did not want the sacrifice of Abraham's son. At the last moment he instructed Abraham to sacrifice a ram in place of Isaac. But it was a supreme test, the test of whether Abraham loved God more than anything or anyone else, and not merely for what God might give to him or do for him. True religion is not doing good in hope of reward, but an open commitment made to God in faith and obedience. In later times the Israelites told the story of Abraham and Isaac to explain why they did not practise human sacrifice, and ultimately the prophets make it clear that God does not want any human sacrifice at all [**Micah 6:7–8**].

Sacrifice

Several times in the stories of the patriarchs we read of how they offered sacrifice. Not only does Abraham nearly sacrifice his son and then sacrifice a ram in his stead, but he, and later on Isaac and Jacob, sacrificed sheep and oxen on many other occasions as well. Sacrifice is important throughout the whole of the Hebrew Scriptures—from the simple sacrifices offered by the patriarchs on altars they built themselves, to the extremely elaborate sacrifices offered much later at the temple in Jerusalem.

What were the reasons for offering sacrifice? First of all, at least in the early days of the Hebrew Scriptures, people offered sacrifice whenever they killed an animal to eat. Meat was a luxury and only eaten on special occasions. Whenever it was eaten, it was treated like a religious act, and people gave thanks to God at the same time. There were, however, special kinds of sacrifices. We can find details of them in **Leviticus 1–7**. Perhaps two of the most important kinds of sacrifice are the 'peace-offering' and the 'sin-offering'. The 'peace-offering' was shared by former enemies as a symbol that hostilities were now over. They were 'at peace'. Perhaps Jacob shared a peace-offering with Esau after they were reconciled. The 'sin-offering' was considered to be a way of removing guilt whenever one had broken any of God's laws or commandments. The offering of the animal, which was given totally to God, was a way of expressing sorrow for the sin committed.

The sacrifice of Isaac

When Abraham tried to sacrifice Isaac, was Isaac aware of what was going on? How old was Isaac at the time? Was he a willing sacrifice? These are the kinds of questions we would very much like to be able to answer. The Hebrew Scriptures tantalisingly, do not tell us, and so people have wondered about this ever since they first read Genesis 22. Eventually later writers—outside the Bible—began to provide us with some answers. After doing their sums, they decided that Isaac must have been 37 years old at the time, and, yes, he very definitely knew what was happening. He was willing to be sacrificed so that the sins of any of his descendants might be forgiven.

In New Testament times, the early Christians also knew the story of Abraham and Isaac. So when they thought about Jesus Christ and his death, they compared this with the sacrifice of Isaac. Jesus was a 'new Isaac' and God the Father was like Abraham who was willing to sacrifice his only son.

God's covenant with Abraham

Read Genesis 15:1–21

The story of Abraham and Isaac in Genesis 22 concludes with a message from God to Abraham: 'I make a vow by my own name—the LORD is speaking—that I will richly bless you. Because you did this and did not keep back your only son from me, I promise that I will give you as many descendants as there are stars in the sky or grains of sand along the seashore. Your descendants shall conquer their enemies. All the nations of the earth will ask me to bless them as I have blessed your descendants—all because you obeyed my command.' [**Genesis 22:16–18**]. This message is a reaffirmation of the agreement God had made with Abraham several years before, shortly after Abraham had arrived in the land of Canaan. This agreement had been a promise by God that he would give him land and many descendants, two things that were highly desirable to a nomadic wanderer like Abraham. God also promised that Abraham would be a source of blessing for all the peoples of the world. The New Testament believes that this promise was finally fulfilled when Jesus Christ came. He was a descendant of Abraham, and as a result of Jesus' life and death all humankind was indeed blessed.

The promise God made to Abraham was an especially solemn agreement. In Genesis 15:18 it is called a *covenant*. 'Covenant' is an extremely important term throughout the Bible. God makes covenants with a variety of individuals, such as Abraham, Noah [**Genesis 9:8**], or David [**2 Samuel 7**]. Sometimes he makes a covenant with a whole nation, as he did with Moses and the Israelites at Mount Sinai. Many years later Christians saw the death of Jesus Christ is seen as a 'new covenant', a new agreement between God and man. Covenant is such an important biblical term that eventually it is used to describe the two halves of the Christian Bible. The word 'testament' is just an alternative way of saying 'covenant', so in fact the Christian Bible is divided into 'the Old Covenant' and 'the New Covenant'.

The covenant that God makes with Abraham is very solemn indeed. First of all, God asks Abraham to cut up some animals. Then a deep sleep falls upon Abraham and, while he is asleep, a flaming torch passes between the cut-up animals. The flaming torch is really a pictorial way of speaking of God himself. Why did God pass between the parts of the animals? It was a way of pledging himself as solemnly as possible to keep his promise to Abraham. When any people who made an agreement walked between specially killed animals, they took upon themselves a curse—a curse that they would be like dead animals if they failed to keep the agreement. It was such a curse that God took upon himself when the burning torch passed between the pieces. That was how seriously God took his covenant with Abraham.

The meeting with God

Read Genesis 32:22–32

After Abraham's death Isaac remained in the land of Canaan. He had not married a Canaanite woman, but a relative of his, Rebecca, who had come all the way from Haran to marry him. Isaac and Rebecca had two sons, Jacob and

Esau. They were completely unlike in character and appearance, and did not get on at all well. However, when we hear of the quarrels between Jacob and Esau we should remember that we are also really hearing the reflection of the conflicts that existed later between the Edomites, the descendants of Esau, and the Israelites, the descendants of Jacob.

Eventually Jacob tricked Esau out of the birthright that really belonged to Esau as the first-born son. He had to flee for his life to escape Esau's anger, and journeyed back to Haran to work for Laban, his mother's brother. He spent many years in Haran and finally married Laban's two daughters, Leah and Rachel. Eventually, though, it was time to return to Canaan, for that was the land of the promise made to Abraham, and Jacob was now the heir to this promise. He journeyed back to Canaan with some fear, for he wondered how Esau would greet him. Just before he was to meet Esau once more he had a very strange experience. He was at the fords of Penuel on the River Jabbok and it was night. He was alone, for he had sent his wives and children on ahead. A man set upon him and began to wrestle with

Jacob pretended he was Esau, Isaac's elder son, so that Isaac (now blind) gave him the blessing that really belonged to the first-born son. Once given, a blessing could not be taken back, even though Jacob had got it dishonestly! As we can imagine, Esau was furious with Jacob (Genesis 27).

As Jacob travelled through Haran to escape Esau's anger, he stopped at a place called Bethel. During the night he had a dream. He saw a stairway stretching from earth to heaven, with angels standing on it. God spoke to him and promised to protect him, even in a foreign land. Later, the Israelites built an important temple at Bethel. (Genesis 28:10–17)

him. He was extremely powerful and Jacob could not overcome him. Eventually the stranger wounded Jacob, but Jacob still refused to give up. He hung on to the strange man and carried on wrestling till the break of day. With the coming of the light, Jacob realised who it was he had wrestled with—an angel of God, or perhaps even God himself. And before the angel disappeared he gave Jacob a new name— 'Israel', which is especially appropriate, for its meaning is 'The one who strives with God'.

Israel

Throughout this book the name Israel will be important. We shall see how it grows in meaning—from describing one man, it eventually describes a whole nation. But throughout the history of 'Israel', one thing remains the same— Israel can never avoid God, Israel must always take God seriously. Sometimes this means wrestling with God at the fords of Jabbok and being wounded in the struggle. Sometimes it means being faithful to God and keeping his laws and commandments, whatever the cost. But one thing is certain: without God, there is no Israel!

4 Down to the land of Egypt

Out of the land of Canaan

Read Genesis 37, 42–45:16

When we speak of Abraham, Isaac and Jacob, we can say they 'sojourned' in the land of Canaan. The word 'sojourn' implies a sort of temporary residence, for it was not yet the time for Abraham's descendants to live permanently in the land. That was to come later, after the Exodus. It is also clear that, though the patriarchs lived among the Canaanites, they did not become part of Canaanite society. They did not marry Canaanite women, for example. As we have already seen, Abraham found a wife for his son Isaac *not* from the land of Canaan, but from among his father's relatives back in Haran **[Genesis 24]**. In turn, so also did Jacob. It was not so much a case of racial prejudice, rather the patriarchs were afraid that, if their sons married women from the land of Canaan, they would start worshipping the gods of the Canaanites, and so be unfaithful to the God who had guided them in their long journeying. In a similar way, in the New Testament Christians are urged not to marry non-believers, since to do so would make it more difficult for them to continue to be Christians.

During Jacob's lifetime he and his family moved down from Canaan into Egypt. There

Joseph's life was a series of 'downs' and 'ups'. Sold into slavery by his brothers, falsely accused by his master's wife, he is thrown into prison. But God is still with him! Joseph interprets dreams, and Pharaoh puts him in charge of the famine relief programme. His brothers come from Canaan, Joseph reveals who he is and at last is reunited with his fathers. Thus God managed to bring good out of evil (Genesis 50:20).

were several reasons for this move. It had begun with a family quarrel—the other brothers' being bitterly jealous of Joseph, whom they regarded as their father's favourite. They took the opportunity one day to seize Joseph and sell him as a slave to traders who were going to Egypt. But there Joseph was eventually to flourish. Through his ability to interpret dreams and thus predict the future, he reached a position of high authority in the land, becoming what we might describe as 'prime minister'. He forgave his brothers and helped and encouraged them to settle in Egypt. For the brothers had not prospered as well as Joseph. There had been several years of poor rainfall in Canaan, and Jacob and his sons had been particularly harshly affected by the famine that had resulted. As 'sojourners' they were the first to suffer when there was not enough to go round. So they were extremely glad to be able to move into Egypt and thus escape the worst of the famine. Throughout the second millennium, nomadic groups did move into Egypt from time to time to find food and pasture.

The land of the Nile

What kind of land did Joseph and his brothers come to? Along with Mesopotamia, Egypt was the oldest civilisation in the ancient world. Civilisation developed in both countries for similar reasons. In Egypt, as in Mesopotamia, there is hardly any rainfall. The people who live there are therefore completely dependent on the waters of the great river Nile which run through the land. The Nile is the source of life for Egypt, as the rivers Tigris and Euphrates are for Mesopotamia. But using a river to provide water for growing crops means developing artificial irrigation schemes. In turn, to design irrigation schemes means that people have to learn to work together. This cooperation born of necessity in both Egypt and Mesopotamia was the initial impetus that led to the building of settlements, towns and eventually cities. Cooperation was doubly necessary, because both in Egypt and Mesopotamia the rivers flooded every year. If the rivers were not controlled by an elaborate drainage system, the whole countryside would have quickly become a marshy chaos.

By the time that Jacob's sons arrived in Egypt we are talking about a very sophisticated culture. The capital of the country was at a city called Avaris in the Nile delta. From here the Egyptian king ruled over a vast area of land which included not only Egypt itself, but frequently extended to include Canaan and lands even further north. Pharaoh (the title of the Egyptian king) did not bother to rule over Canaan himself directly. Instead he used vassal kings, each of whom ruled over a few cities. The vassal promised to be loyal to his overlord Pharaoh and to pay him the appropriate sum in tribute. In return, Pharaoh agreed to support the vassal, especially whenever danger threatened.

We have a series of letters called the Tell el-Amarna letters that form part of the correspondence between the court of Pharaoh and these vassal kings of Canaan. The Tell el-Amarna letters make it quite clear that Pharaoh did not always live up to his promises! One vassal king, from the city of Byblos, complains that he is shut up by his enemies like 'a bird that lies in a net' and that Pharaoh has not sent

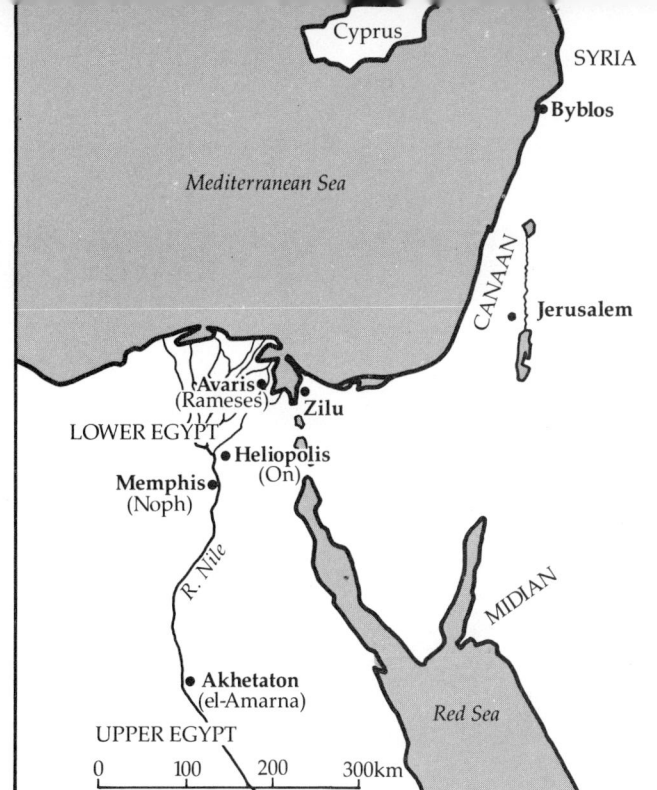

any help. Other Tell el-Amarna letters come from Jerusalem. There the vassal king Abdi-Hepa refers to the desperate situation he is facing at the hands of Pharaoh's enemies, and pleads 'do not abandon the lands of Jerusalem'.

These Tell el-Amarna letters come from somewhat after the time of Joseph, when the Egyptian Empire was in a period of political instability. However, at the time when Joseph and his brothers went down to Egypt—probably the seventeenth century BC—the empire of the Egyptians was still in its full glory. Egyptian armies went on strenuous military campaigns that took them far from their homeland. Egyptian trade and commerce also flourished. Horses and precious stones came from Babylon. From Cyprus copper was sent (the word Cyprus actually means 'copper-land'); iron came from north Syria, and cedar wood from the city of Byblos. In return, Egypt would send gold and silver and sometimes the reeds of the papyrus plant, which grew in Egypt and could be stuck together to make material for writing on. Then there was granite from Aswan on the Upper Nile, much prized for the making of monuments. The riches that came from trade and empire were used to build and furnish splendid temples and palaces, of which the remains today still speak of their magnificence.

19

The world of the scribes

It was not just for their physical splendour that the courts of Pharaoh were famed. In and around the palaces of the land revolved an immense and complicated bureaucracy. The like of it was not to be seen anywhere else in the ancient world. The story of Joseph gives us a taste of what we mean when we speak of the 'bureaucracy' of Ancient Egypt. There were prime ministers, secretaries of state, royal heralds, stewards, tax officials, military officers, an elaborate priesthood. In a letter written in the fourteenth century BC we can read of 'performers of manual labour and office jobs, magistrates commanding administrators, chief major-domo, mayor, headmen of villages, quartermaster . . . chief of departments, scribe of the offering-table, controllers, retainer, messenger of administrators, brewer, baker, butler, butcher, servant, confectioner, baker of cakes, butler tasting the wine, chief of works, overseer of carpenters, chief craftsman, deputy, draughtsman, sculptor, miner, quarryman, demolisher, stone-worker . . . barber, basket maker.' It was a far cry from the simple and uncomplicated way of life that Abraham and his family knew while they were nomadic wanderers.

At the top level of what might be best described as 'Pharaoh's civil service' was a class of people who went by the general name of 'scribes'. Officials like the prime minister and the secretary of state would come from this scribal class. The word 'scribe' means a 'writer', and that is the clue to the complicated working of the Egyptian civil service.

All the potential 'higher grade' civil servants went to 'scribal school' where they learnt the art of writing. This was a complicated and lengthy business with the hieroglyphs of Ancient Egypt. When they had become sufficiently competent in this skill to satisfy their teachers, they went on to the next stage of their education, which was to learn 'wisdom'. Learning 'wisdom' involved the study of what we would call arithmetic, geography, letter composition, botany and zoology. Perhaps it also included the interpretation of dreams, bookkeeping and business studies. However, its most important component was the advice given by the teacher to his pupils on 'How to succeed in life'. This included elements of morality—though these were of a fairly practical nature. If you look at the Book of Proverbs in the Hebrew Scriptures you can get a good idea of the practical and pragmatic wisdom taught in the scribal schools. When the student had finally graduated, he then could expect to work his way up through the government bureaucracy, perhaps one day arriving at the very top. But, however far up the ladder he managed to climb, he never had any doubt in his mind that he had chosen the best profession of all. Among the textbooks in the scribal schools were several volumes that listed the possible professions and jobs open to people. After going through the hardships involved in being a soldier, a farmer, a merchant or a sailor, they invariably end with the advice, 'If you have any sense, be a scribe'!

Pharaoh: the god-man

Far above all other mortals in his kingdom was Pharaoh. In fact, he was not really considered to be a mortal at all. Ancient Egyptian religion was polytheistic (it had many gods). Each town in the country had its own local god or goddess.

Many of these were represented as animals—for example, there was the cat goddess Bast worshipped at Bubastis, and the jackal god Wepawet at Lycopolis. Besides these local gods there were national gods associated with the sun and with the Nile, since the sun and the Nile affected the life of every Egyptian. The name of the Nile god was Hopi, while the sun god was called Ra (Re). The pharaohs were closely associated with the god Ra. Each of the Pharaohs in turn was considered to be Ra's son, perhaps even Ra himself in a visible form. And after his death the Pharaoh was considered to be divine and so was worshipped. Often his name showed his connection with Ra. There were, for example, several pharaohs called Rameses, a name which means 'Ra has given'.

Egypt was, therefore, a new and very different world—unlike anything they had previously encountered—to which Jacob and his sons came from the land of Canaan.

The god Osiris being worshipped by a high priest.

Hieroglyphs

As in Mesopotamia, writing in Egypt was an elaborate art. The language was not the same as in Mesopotamia, nor was the script, but it was just as difficult to learn! Ancient Egyptian writing was known as *hieroglyphic*. It was made up of a large number of picture-symbols which were sometimes read horizontally, and at other times from top to bottom. Hieroglyphic writing is significant because it reminds us just what all writing originally was—an attempt to represent the world around us and to communicate it to other people. Originally, of course, things were represented by symbols as like them in shape as possible. The sun, for example, was a round disc. Gradually, however, the symbols used in writing became increasingly stylised and most unlike the things they were trying to describe.

Egyptian hieroglyphic writing represents quite an early stage in this development. It is still a form of picture-writing, but the pictures are almost a kind of code. For example, just how do you represent verbs when you are using picture-writing? The Egyptians' solution was to use a large number of different birds, but then the business of writing immediately became that much more complicated. Eventually, Egyptian hieroglyphic writing had about as many different symbols as the Mesopotamian cuneiform. Once again this meant that only one class in society—the scribal class—learnt to read and write. Both in Egypt and in Mesopotamia the difficulty of learning to read and write the language deeply affected the nature of the society and civilisation. This contrasts with the much more 'democratic' and simpler language that was eventually used by the Israelites.

5   The pharaohs who knew not Joseph

The Hyksos

There may also be another reason which would help account for the settlement in Egypt of Jacob and his sons. Egyptian texts from this period refer to a group of people they call the 'Hyksos'. These Hyksos suddenly became extremely powerful in Egypt. The texts make it clear that the Hyksos were not native Egyptians. They seem to have come from another part of the Middle East and to have invaded Egypt. The Hyksos were a semitic people. This means that they would have been of the same racial group as Abraham and his descendants. It is quite likely that Joseph's rise to power and the move of Jacob and his family to Egypt was made much easier because of the rule of Hyksos kings in Egypt. They would naturally favour and assist fellow foreigners, particularly if they were of a semitic race. Once again we seem to

have a case of God working through political and social movements and changes, and using them to bring about his purposes. Indeed, the story of Joseph and his brothers makes it clear that this is precisely how God *does* work.

The good times for Jacob's descendants in Egypt did not last very long. Perhaps a hundred years after the family of Jacob went to Egypt, the political situation in the country altered dramatically. The Hyksos kings who had been much resented in Egypt were driven out and a native Egyptian dynasty of Pharoahs took their place. As we might imagine, the Israelites who had arrived in Egypt as protégés of the Hyksos kings were very unpopular with the new rulers. Gradually their position altered from that of welcome guests—they became instead forced labourers. They had come to Egypt to find refuge, and now they were not free to go.

Scenes from a frieze in the tomb of Rekh-mi-Re depicting labourers at work on a building project. Other friezes show hungry nomads coming to Egypts for food. How many of them ended up, like the Israelites, as slave labourers?

The Hebrew slaves

Read Exodus 1

According to the Book of Exodus, these Pharaohs 'who knew not Joseph', and who did not remember how Joseph's wisdom and prudence had saved Egypt from disaster, set the Israelites to work on a building project of immense proportions. The task assigned was to build two store-cities for Pharaoh, Pithom and Rameses [**Exodus 1:11**]. The Israelites were particularly suitable for this task, for they had settled in the land of Goshen, in the eastern part of the Nile delta. This was precisely where the store-cities needed to be built.

During the centuries that they lived in Egypt, the Israelites must have adopted many of the customs of the Egyptians. Yet at the same time they seem to have managed to keep their distinct and separate identity. Perhaps the fact that they lived in the land of Goshen helped here, since this was the part of Egypt nearest to the desert on the east, and we can imagine that a certain amount of 'traffic' of nomadic peoples continued back and forth across the boundaries of Egypt. This would have helped the Israelites stay in touch with their nomadic roots. During the early chapters of Exodus, the Israelites are often called 'Hebrews'. This reminds us of Abraham who, as we have already seen (section 2), was called the 'Hebrew'. Here once again Hebrew seems to be a rather negative word and refers to the low status of the Israelites in Egypt. The Egyptians regarded them both as outsiders and as slaves. We are also reminded of the similarity with the Habiru mentioned in writings outside the Bible. In fact, there are actually documents from Egypt that refer to Habiru slaves being used on city building projects. So the connection between the Habiru and the Biblical Hebrews does seem to be very close indeed.

What was the name of the Pharaoh who forced the Israelites to become his slave-labourers? The Hebrew Scriptures actually do not tell us. That might seem strange to us, but it is characteristic of the way in which the Hebrew Scriptures tell history—they concentrate on they central purpose and omit details that they consider irrelevant to that purpose, even if we would find them interesting. The purpose

Statues of Rameses II, who was probably the Pharaoh of the Exodus, at Abu Simbel in Egypt.

of Exodus 1 and 2 is to provide a backcloth and set the stage in a way that will highlight the marvellous power and care of God of which the writer will tell us later. For this purpose the name of one particular Pharaoh is rather irrelevant—so we are not told it!

All the same, by looking closely at Egyptian records we can make a guess that the building of the store-cities was probably begun by the Pharaoh Seti I (about 1305–1290 BC) and continued under his son Rameses II (about 1290–1224 BC). You will remember that **Exodus 1:11** names Rameses as one of the cities that the Israelites built—this was a city that had originally been called Avaris, and had once upon a time been the capital of Egypt. But after the Hyksos had been expelled, the Egyptians had moved the capital to a city called Thebes in Upper Egypt. Now Seti and Rameses wanted to move the capital back to the delta area, since one of their priorities was to try and regain control of the land of Canaan, a control which the Tell el-Amarna letters imply had previously been lost. So they rebuilt Avaris, and Rameses named it after himself.

The baby in the bulrushes

Read Exodus 2:1–10

This harsh labour was apparently not enough. The day came when Pharaoh decreed that, in order to prevent the Israelites becoming too numerous, their male children should be killed at birth. The brutal command led to anguish among the Hebrews. One mother, Jochabed, determined that at all costs her newborn son should have the chance to live. For some months after his birth she successfully hid him. Eventually he grew too big—and cried too loudly—to be safely concealed, and then she placed him in a basket of bulrushes and hid him along the banks of one of the streams of the Nile. There was at least a chance that the baby would be found and rescued by one of the Egyptians. And that is what happened. It was the daughter of Pharaoh herself who came upon the baby as she went to bathe in the river. Although she realised he was a Hebrew child, she made up her mind to rear the baby. She decided to find a foster mother for the baby from among the Hebrew women, and in doing so, unwittingly gave him back to Jochabed. That was not such a coincidence! Jochabed had had the forethought to send Miriam, the baby's sister, to the river to keep an eye on what would happen. Miriam therefore was in the right place at the right time to suggest Jochabed as the foster mother.

The story of the birth and upbringing of Moses has some elements of folklore about it. People always enjoy telling tales of great men, and how they come from very lowly backgrounds. There was a very similar story told about Sargon, who was once upon a time King of Mesopotamia. He too was born in secret, placed in a basket of bulrushes, and set adrift on the river—and eventually he became a great ruler. So it is possible that in the story of Moses' birth the drama and suspense has been heightened by the addition of elements from the traditional folklore about the birth of great men. However, the core of the tale is surely reliable. Moses the leader of the Israelites, who was to liberate them from their slavery in Egypt and guide them through the wilderness, undoubtedly had Egyptian connections. His name itself indicates this. For 'Moses' is the second half of an Egyptian-style name, from which the first half is missing. It is similar in form to 'Tutmoses' which means 'the god Tut gave' or 'Rameses' which means 'the god Ra gave'. (Compare names we use today, such as 'Jonathan' which means 'the Lord gave'.) Most probably while Moses was growing up as the foster child of Pharaoh's daughter his name was something like Tutmoses or Rameses. When, however, he became the leader of the Israelites, the 'Tut' or 'Ra' was dropped, leaving plain 'Moses'. This was felt to be more appropriate for the man who was to lead his people once again to worship the God of their fathers.

The splendour of the sun

A hundred years or so before the time of Moses there was a young Pharaoh who had some startling new ideas. He wanted to do away with the traditional polytheistic religion of the Egyptians and worship one god alone—the sun disc called Aton. The Pharaoh was called Akhenaton, a significant name because it means 'Servant of Aton', and his enthusiasm knew no limits as he tried to enforce Aton-worship throughout his lands. Among other things, Akhenaton was responsible for a beautful hymn, called 'the Hymn to the Aton' which praises the sun-disc for the care with which it watches over all people in all lands.

Because Akhenaton's reform occurred fairly shortly before Moses was born, people have sometimes wondered whether he was influenced by it in any way. Akhenaton insisted on worshipping one god, and so later on did Moses. However, sadly perhaps, Akhenaton's reform was extremely unpopular with his people, and after his death they quickly returned to their more traditional worship of the many gods of Egypt. This makes it unlikely that Moses was greatly affected by the ideas of Akhenaton as he grew up at the court of the Pharaohs.

Bust of Akhenaton, the Pharaoh who worshipped 'one god'. Could his belief have influenced the Israelites?

Relief sculpture of the sun's rays (Aton), with the figures of Akhenaton and Nefertiti chipped out by the old priesthood they had tried to replace.

6 I am who I am

Although Moses was brought up as a wealthy Egyptian, he was obviously aware of his Hebrew and Israelite background, and it was with the Israelites that he identified when the moment came. One day, seeing an Egyptian overseer beating a Hebrew labourer, he went to the labourer's help and accidentally killed the Egyptian. He had hoped that no-one had seen the killing, but soon afterwards he realised that what he had done was being widely talked about. Moses fled, in fear of his life.

The land of Midian

Read Exodus 3:1–15
Moses fled to a country referred to in the Hebrew Scriptures as 'the land of Midian'. There he met the priest of the Midianites, who seems to have had two names—Reuel and Jethro—and he married his daughter. The Midianites were a people of the same sort of background as the Israelites, nomadic people keeping sheep and goats and seeking pasture for them. The Hebrew Scriptures imply the Midianites were distantly related to the Israelites—Midian, the founder of the tribe, being a son of Abraham, not by Sarah but by another wife whom he married after Sarah's death. It was therefore appropriate for the Midianites to welcome Moses among them, and for a while he became a shepherd, helping to keep the flocks of his father-in-law.

One day, as Moses was pasturing the flocks, he came to a mountain called Horeb, 'the mountain of God'. The story continues: 'There the angel of the LORD appeared to him as a flame coming from the middle of a bush. Moses saw that the bush was on fire but that it was not burning up. "This is strange," he thought. "Why isn't the bush burning up? I will go closer and see." When the LORD saw that Moses was coming closer, he called to him from the middle of the bush and said, "Moses, Moses!" He answered, "Yes, here I am." God said, "Do not

come any closer. Take off your sandals, because you are standing on holy ground. I am the God of your ancestors, the God of Abraham, Isaac and Jacob." So Moses covered his face, because he was afraid to look at God.'

The mountain of God

Where was this 'mountain of God', Mount Horeb? First, we should note that Mount Horeb is the same mountain that is called Mount Sinai in other chapters of Exodus. Two different traditions in the Bible have used two different names for the same mountain (see the box below).

Since the fourth century AD, Jewish and Christian tradition has located Sinai/Horeb near the southern tip of the great peninsula which lies to the east of Egypt and is known today as 'the Sinai peninsula'. A monastery has been built there, sheltering underneath a tremendous mountain called Jebel Musa. Jebel Musa, which is the Arabic way of saying 'Mount Moses', is certainly considered to be Mount Sinai/Horeb by the many thousands of pilgrims who have visited and climbed the 2300 metres up the mountain. It is at least reasonable to think that Jebel Musa may be the Mount Sinai/Horeb of the Bible. However, there are some people who consider that the descriptions given of Mount Sinai later in Exodus [**Exodus 19:16–19**], of cloud and of thundering, imply that the biblical Mount Sinai was a volcano. If this is so, then Jebel Musa cannot have been Mount Sinai, since Jebel Musa is not a volcano, either active or extinct. Indeed, if Mount Sinai was a volcano, it cannot have been located in the Sinai Peninsula at all, since this has no volcanoes. It must then have been further east in the northern part of the great land mass called Arabia, where there are several volcanoes. If we could be sure where exactly the 'land of Midian' was, this would help us to locate Mount Sinai—but since the Midianites where a nomadic tribe, their territory could well have included *both* the northern part of Arabia *and* part of the Sinai Peninsula. On balance, there are no definitive arguments against the theory that Jebel Musa, the traditional site, was in fact Mount Sinai.

Mount Sinai at sunrise. Throughout the Bible there are occasions where mountains are the site of important meetings between men and God. Besides Moses, there is also the story of Elijah's visit to Horeb (1 Kings 19). In the New Testament it is on a mountain that Jesus is transfigured (Mark 9) and from a mountain that he ascends to heaven (Acts 1). The height and grandeur of mountains are often said to make people feel closer to God.

The Pentateuch: J,E,D,P

The stories of Moses and the patriarchs were written down several centuries after they took place. Probably several writers, or groups of writers, wrote the story down at different times. Although it was the same story they told, each writer told it in his own way. Eventually the different versions of the story were combined and went to make up the *Pentateuch*. (The Pentateuch is the name given to the first five books of the Hebrew Scriptures: Genesis, Exodus, Leviticus, Numbers and Deuteronomy.) Most scholars think that there were *four* different writers involved in the writing of what is now the Pentateuch. They have given them names as follows:

J—the Jahwist writer who wrote in about 950 BC.
E—the Elohist writer who wrote in about 750 BC.
D—the Deuteronomic writer. His work is found mainly in the Book of Deuteronomy. He wrote in about 700 BC.
P—the Priestly writer who wrote in about 550 BC.

Although we have called them writers, we must not think of them like modern authors, writing a complete book from scratch. Perhaps 'editors' would be a better term for them. In each case they took traditional stories which had previously circulated orally, and set the stories in a framework to make these relevant to the people of their own time. In section 20 we shall see how the J writer used the stories.

It is also important to realise that these writers were most likely not four *individuals*, but groups of people who held the same viewpoint. This is particularly the case with D and P. One of the ways we can check which writer wrote which parts of the Pentateuch is by checking what God is called. For although the E writer and the P writer believed that God revealed his name, Yahweh, only at the time of Moses [**Exodus 6:2–3**], the J writer described God as Yahweh from the beginning of history. So, looking through the Book of Genesis which tells the story of the Israelites before Moses, whenever you see God referred to as Yahweh or 'the LORD', you can be sure that that part of the story is written by the J writer.

Muslim worshippers today remove their shoes as they enter the 'holy ground' of the mosque.

The holy ground

The experience that Moses had at the mountain was of decisive significance for his future and the future of his people. Suddenly he became aware that he was standing on 'holy ground'. When today we use the word 'holy' to describe someone, we may mean more or less the same as 'good'. So a 'holy man' means a 'good man'. There is some truth in this understanding of 'holiness', but it is not the total picture as presented by the Hebrew Scriptures. For when the Hebrew Scriptures use the word 'holy', they do so to refer to things that belong to God and the divine world and therefore are separate from the ordinary realm of human life. Later in their history the Israelites were, rightly, to grasp that holiness and goodness ought to go closely together, but at the time of Moses this was not yet fully understood. When the voice out of the bush told Moses that he was standing on holy ground, it meant that God himself was present and had broken through the barriers that normally separate the divine and the human worlds. God's presence at Horeb is also shown in the mysterious fire that burns in the bush, for in the Hebrew Scriptures fire is often used to describe symbolically the mysterious activity of God [Exodus 13:21]. In the New Testament this is also true, for the Holy Spirit comes to the apostles at Pentecost with tongues of fire.

The nearness of God is also made clear when the writer speaks of Moses' fear. In the ancient world people believed that if someone saw God he or she would inevitably die—for it would be as though he or she had received a strong electric shock [Judges 13:22]. So what the story of Moses at the burning bush is trying to convey to us is that God, normally felt to be separate from us and our world, was not separate at all, but was actually very close to people! And what is more, he had not only come to be with people, but also to *do* and *act* for them. Consider how the story continues, 'Then the LORD said, "I have seen how cruelly my people are being treated in Egypt . . . I know all about their sufferings, and so I have come down to rescue them".' His people's suffering in slavery had clearly been very much on the mind of Moses—it had been the very reason why he had been forced to flee from Egypt. The God whom he met at this holy mountain had revealed himself, not just to show off his power and to terrify Moses, but in order to *be with* and *rescue* his people, the Israelites, from their slavery in the land of Egypt.

A historical faith

Perhaps this is one of the most important things to grasp about the Hebrew Scriptures, or indeed about the Bible as a whole. Again and again throughout the Hebrew Scriptures God acts, God does, God relates to his people, indeed to all people, in history, in events in time and space. Some religions believe and have believed that the greatest religious experience possible is a kind of 'mystical' experience in which the believer escapes from this world and is caught up into the Otherness of God. That is not, however, the Biblical picture. For in the Bible people do not escape to another world. And because God involves himself so closely with people's affairs, his servants must do so as well. The end of the story of the Burning Bush is *not* Moses contemplating mystically the wonder of God. Instead it is Moses being sent back into Egypt, commissioned as God's messenger and spokesman to rescue his people.

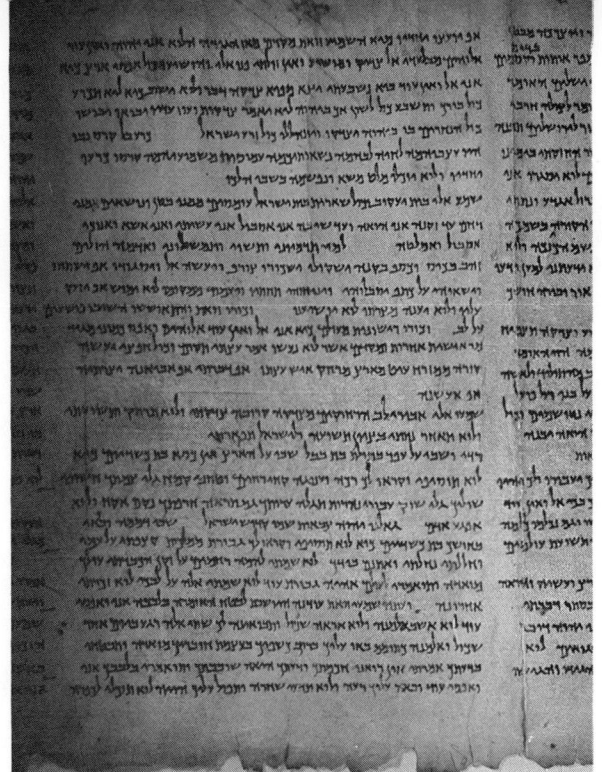

The Dead Sea scrolls are the oldest manuscripts of the Hebrew Scriptures we possess.

The name of God

However, before Moses returns to Egypt, he asks and learns the name of the God who is sending him. One can sense that Moses may be using delaying tactics here—he doesn't really want to go back and is trying to think of every possible reason not to.

When God tells Moses at Mount Sinai what his name is, we are meant to realise that he is letting people in on a very big secret, because Moses was part of a world in which names had a very real significance. Previously the patriarch Jacob had met God and had asked what his name was, but God had refused to tell him [**Genesis 32:29**]. Now God is willing to tell Moses what his name is, and therefore let people know who he really is.

According to **Exodus 3:15**, God's name is made up of the four letters YHWH. The text of the Hebrew Scriptures did not include any vowels for YHWH, but many scholars have suggested that the name was pronounced Yahweh. The word Yahweh is closely related to the verb 'to be' in Hebrew. So when God declared his name to be Yahweh this meant to say that he was the God who 'is', who is the origin and source of all creation and being, and that he

was a God who was ready to 'be with' his people in their trouble. But all the same, a certain mysteriousness remains, and this is deliberate. 'Being' is one of the most difficult ideas for us to understand fully, and in the same way God can never be completely understood by human beings. His thoughts are higher than our thoughts, and he cannot be controlled by those to whom he has graciously revealed his name. In **Exodus 3:14**, God says 'I am who I am', the God who *is* and *does* what *he* alone decides.

In later years the people of the Hebrew Scriptures became very hesitant about saying God's name. So whenever the word Yahweh was written in the Bible they would read out 'Adonai', a Hebrew word that means 'the Lord'. Most of the English translations of the Bible have followed this custom, and have translated Yahweh by the LORD (generally in capital letters). Occasionally Christians also use the word *Jehovah*, which combines the consonants of Yahweh and the vowels of Adonai!

The importance of names

It is difficult for us to grasp fully the significance of what it meant for Moses to learn God's name. There are two reasons for this. First, our faith is *monotheistic*. We worship only one God and we therefore don't need to know his particular and personal name. In the ancient world the situation was very different. Most nations were *polytheistic*: they believed in and worshipped several gods, each of whom had his or her own 'department' or speciality. So it was a very important question to ask of a god, 'Who are you? What is your name?', for it meant 'Which god are you?'

The second reason is connected with what a 'name' meant to the Israelites. If I were an Israelite, I would think that my name was in some mysterious way part of my 'me-ness'. I would believe that the meaning of my name summed up what I essentially was. I wouldn't be at all happy at telling you what my name was, because I would be deeply afraid of your using my name in a magical way to get power over me and make me do what you wanted!

7 Let my people go!

Pharaoh's defeat

Hesitantly, but obediently, Moses returned to Egypt. His commission was to persuade Pharaoh to allow the Israelites to leave Egypt and go and worship Yahweh in the wilderness. Not surprisingly, Pharaoh refused to agree to the idea. In fact, his reaction was to make the Israelites work harder than ever—now they were no longer to be given the straw they needed to make their bricks for building, but they had to go and gather the straw themselves. Also, not surprisingly, the Israelites showed their resentment at this new task by turning on Moses himself—for if he hadn't interfered, this extra burden would not have been laid upon them. In turn Moses protested to Yahweh—his

---

Hardening the heart

When the Book of Exodus states the Yahweh 'hardened the heart' of Pharaoh [**Exodus 4:21**] what does it mean? Is it really saying that Yahweh *deliberately* led Pharaoh to reject the signs which Moses performed, just so that he could inflict still more plagues upon the Egyptians? Does God really work like that? Later on in the Hebrew Scriptures we can find the prophet Isaiah suggesting something similar—the people will not listen to his prophecy because Yahweh had shut their ears and their eyes. Something almost the same is said in the New Testament about the teaching of Jesus himself [**Mark 4:11–12**]. Our understanding of God and his love makes it very difficult for us to believe that God would ever have deliberately hardened people's hearts, so when we meet such passages in the Bible we should remember:

1. Philosophers and scholars have always found it a problem to balance the idea of free will with the idea of a God who is all-powerful. Even though we today believe that people are free to choose good and evil for themselves—God does not do it for them—if we are being entirely consistent, we must admit that this limits the all-powerfulness of God. The Bible preferred to emphasise the all-powerfulness of Yahweh, even if this meant somehow appearing to limit people's free will.

2. In the ancient world people did not distinguish quite as clearly as we do between 'aim' and 'result'. Because the 'result' of the signs was that Pharaoh did not believe and was even more angry than before, this could lead some people to feel that this was also the 'aim' of the signs. God's aim is always to save people, to bring light where darkness has been before. When a light shines in a room, it shows up evil and dirt which has not previously been seen clearly. That is not the aim of putting on the light, but that is what is bound to happen. In the world of the Bible the same is true. The darkness of evil people is shown up more clearly by God's saving light. They themselves will therefore try and turn away from the light. So the aim of God's signs in Egypt was to 'save' Israelites (and Egyptians), but it was inevitable, given Pharaoh's own darkness, that he would turn away and harden his own heart.

mission had failed, and it was no more than he had expected. God's response was to send Moses right back to confront Pharaoh once more, but this time with a helper, his brother Aaron. Aaron was a better speaker than Moses, so he would do the talking. Moses would tell him what to say. And, just in case Pharaoh still refused to let the Israelites go, God promised that he would reinforce his message if necessary with 'signs and wonders'.

The next few chapters of Exodus read like a drama or a play. Again and again Pharaoh refuses to allow the Israelites to leave, and again and again Yahweh responds by performing a 'sign' against Pharaoh and the Egyptians. As the story progresses, the tension and suspense mount—who will win this contest? Will it be Yahweh, with Moses and Aaron? Or will it be Pharaoh and his magicians? Finally there comes the last sign—the death of the first-born sons of the Egyptians. Pharaoh is defeated, Yahweh has won. The Israelites can go, set free by Yahweh's mighty arm.

The hailstorm and the swarm of frogs—after ten such plagues, the Egyptians had had enough and let the Israelites go.

The ten signs

The drama that lies in the Biblical account of these 'signs' **[Exodus 7:14–12;36]** is not accidental. After the escape from Egypt, throughout the rest of their history, each year the Israelites remembered the marvellous way Yahweh had struggled on their behalf. It may even be that they acted out, each year, as a kind of religious drama, the contest between Yahweh and Pharaoh. This would have influenced the way the story was told and retold, and finally how it was written down to appear in the Hebrew Scriptures.

The contest between Yahweh and Pharaoh involves ten 'signs', often called the Ten Plagues, although the word 'plague' actually does not appear very often in the biblical story. They are:

1. The turning of the waters of the Nile into blood
2. A swarm of frogs which comes from the Nile and creates havoc in Egypt
3. Swarms of gnats
4. Clouds of flies
5. A plague which affects the cattle of the Egyptians
6. Boils and sores that break out on people and animals
7. A tremendous hailstorm
8. Swarms of locusts
9. Darkness over the land for three days
10. The death of the first-born sons of the Egyptians

All these events, except the last one, are things which could and did—and still do—happen from time to time in the Nile valley. For example, during the flood season the waters of the Nile can turn reddish through all the red soil that is washed down from upstream. Swarms of gnats, frogs, flies and locusts regularly cause devastation in Egypt and other parts of the Middle East. Every year in the spring there are winds that blow in from the desert. They bring with them a large amount of sand, and this can obscure the sun. This desert wind, known by the peoples of the near east as the khamsin or sirocco, can often last for several days. So most of the 'plagues' could be described as natural phenomena.

A swarm of locusts in present-day Sudan. Locusts still ravage many parts of the fertile lands in North Africa.

Miracles and signs

In the twentieth century, whenever we think about miracles, we also think about 'natural law'. We expect the world and the universe to behave in certain clearly defined ways. Perhaps some of us might compare God to a clockmaker who makes a clock, winds it up and sets it going. We think that God's clock, the universe, does not need further assistance from him once it has been wound up—it will continue ticking away by itself, working under its own system, i.e. natural law. If we look at the universe in this way, it means we regard a 'miracle' as an exceptional event, a disruption of natural law. It is as if God has suddenly decided to interfere with the clock which normally he lets run completely by itself. However, in the Hebrew Scriptures writers did not look at the world as we do—and this means also that they do not look at miracles quite as we do. For the writers of the Bible the world was most definitely *not* a clock that ran by itself once it had been wound up. God was involved in his world all the time—in everything—in making the rain fall, in the birth of a child. The world of the Bible did not make the same distinction we do between 'natural' and 'supernatural' events. Both were seen as 'acts of God'.

This is important to remember when we look at the story of the Ten Plagues. They are indeed 'signs'—the Bible much prefers the word 'sign' to the word 'miracle'. But in the Hebrew Scriptures, events which seem quite ordinary are called 'signs' as well as events that we would call miraculous. Both are 'signs', for whether miraculous or quite ordinary they show us the kind of God that Yahweh is—a God who is close at hand and deeply involved in his people's life and history. In other words the '*sig*nificance' of '*signs*' is that they proclaim in a very direct way that God *is* right here in this world he made and controls. Many years after the time of Moses, the prophet Isaiah walked naked and barefoot in the streets of Jerusalem for three years [Isaiah 20:1–6]—this was a 'sign' that Yahweh would send nations into slavery, when they would be carried off naked and barefoot; a 'sign', but hardly a miracle.

The other thing we need to notice about biblical 'signs' is that they are only seen as such by those who have eyes to see. Signs do not *compel* faith. Rather they can only be properly understood by those who already have trust and faith. The ten signs that Moses caused to happen did not lead Pharaoh to worship Yahweh—far from it, he was just glad to see the Israelites go and not have anything more to do with the strange god, Yahweh. On the other hand, as the Israelites looked back with gratitude on the way God had guided them out of Egypt, they saw in quite ordinary things, perhaps a khamsin or a swarm of locusts, the hand of God at work bringing about his purpose. (See also *Jesus and the Gospels* in this series.)

The Passover

Read Exodus 12:21–32

The final sign, a Black Death that kills the eldest sons of the Egyptians, is linked with the keeping of the Passover feast. Each of the families of the Israelites was instructed to sacrifice a lamb and smear its blood on the doorposts of their house. All the houses of the Israelites were then 'passed over' and the sons of the Israelites were spared from death. The blood of the lambs became a substitute for them, just as the ram had been a substitute for Isaac. It seems quite likely that the custom of killing lambs each year went back among the Israelites for many years before the time of Moses. Probably it was a custom known even to Abraham while he was wandering as a nomad, centuries earlier. Each spring the Israelites—and other nomadic people—ate a lamb and sprinkled its blood on the entrance to their tents to stop demons or evil spirits from coming too near and destroying either people or flocks. It was a ritual that was observed in the spring-time, because that was the time of year when the nomads would be suddenly preparing to go and look for new summer pastures, and they wanted to make sure they would be safe on what might be a long and difficult journey.

At the time of Moses this ancient custom was given a new meaning. Now whenever the Passover sacrifice of lambs was made by the Israelites, whether as they journeyed in the desert or after they settled in the land of Canaan, they remembered God's great action in freeing them from slavery in Egypt. 'When your children ask you, "What does this ritual mean?" You will answer, It is the sacrifice of the Passover to honour the LORD, because he passed over the houses of the Israelites in Egypt. He killed the Egyptians, but spared us.' These words from **Exodus 12:27** are still used today by the Jewish people as they celebrate the Passover each year. As we shall see once again in section 11, it is characteristic of the faith of Israel to take over festivals celebrated by many people in the ancient Middle East and make them particularly their own, particularly Israelite, by linking them with their own historical faith. In turn, at a much later time, the Christian Church 'took over' several Jewish festivals and linked them with historical events that happened during the birth of the Church. In fact the most important Jewish festival to be taken over by the early Church was Passover. The early Christians linked it to Easter, for they saw Christ as their Passover Lamb who had been slain. They believed his death had freed them from slavery—not now from physical slavery in Egypt—but from the equally real slavery to sin.

The Passover, celebrated by Jewish people each year, recalls the Exodus from Egypt. It is a big festival for all the family.

8 The victory at the sea

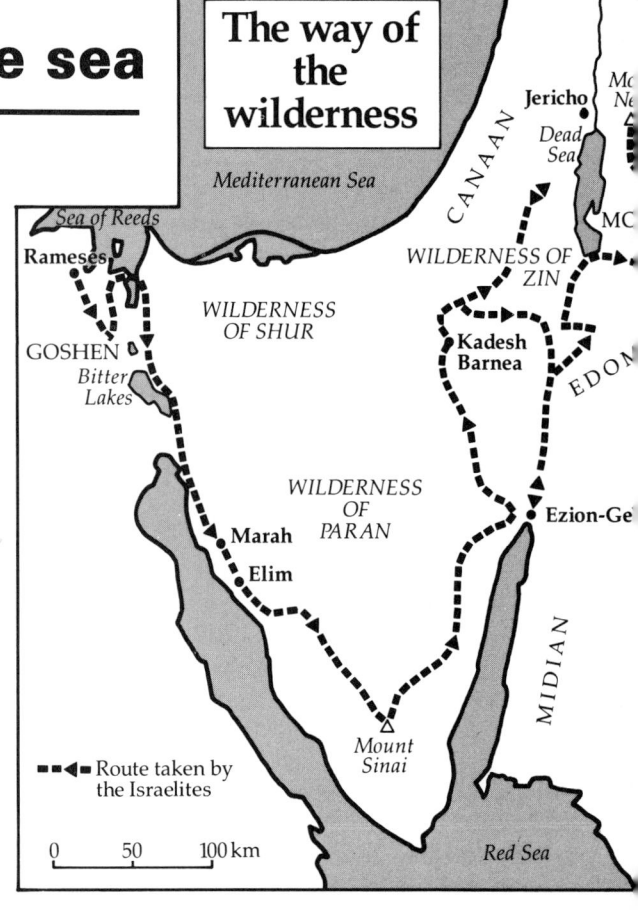

The way of the wilderness

Mediterranean Sea

Sea of Reeds

Rameses

GOSHEN

Bitter Lakes

WILDERNESS OF SHUR

Marah

Elim

WILDERNESS OF PARAN

Mount Sinai

CANAAN

Jericho

Dead Sea

WILDERNESS OF ZIN

Kadesh Barnea

EDOM

Ezion-Ge

MIDIAN

Red Sea

■■◀■ Route taken by the Israelites

0   50   100 km

After the final sign—the death of the eldest sons in each of the Egyptian families—Pharaoh agreed to allow the Israelites to leave Egypt. He did so unwillingly and was soon to change his mind. It seems that the Israelites were aware of this possibility, for their preparations to leave were made secretly and as hurriedly as possible. Although they had only requested permission from Pharaoh to make a three days' journey into the wilderness to worship Yahweh, they fully intended never to come back once they had escaped from Egypt. Instead they meant to make their way round to the land of Canaan where their ancestors had lived for several generations before coming to Egypt. With this in mind they needed to decide upon their route from Egypt to Canaan.

The way of the wilderness

At first sight it appears strange that the Israelites did not go the most direct way which kept close to the coast, 'the way of the land of the Philistines' [Exodus 13:17]. This was the easiest route between Egypt and Canaan; indeed it was part of a 'main road' that led from Egypt and reached all the way to Mesopotamia. But that was the problem. Precisely because it was such an important route there were many Egyptian frontier fortresses located all the way along it—so if the Israelites had decided to travel that way, they would surely have had to fight many battles with Egyptian soldiers. So instead they took a much longer route, 'the way of the wilderness' [Exodus 13:18], which led south-east from Egypt. There was also another important reason. Moses actually did want to take the Israelites to worship Yahweh at Mount Sinai, 'the mountain of God', to thank him for making this escape possible. If we assume that the traditional site of Mount Sinai, Jebel Musa, is the correct site (see section 6), then the route of the Israelites is shown by the dotted line on the map on this page.

As they escaped from Egypt, the Israelites were, as Moses expected, pursued by the Egyptian army. Suddenly they found themselves in an impossible situation. In front of them was a body of water which stopped them in their tracks. But they could not go back, or else they would have to face the Egyptians and their army. The people complained, as at so many other times, to Moses. They said that it would have been better if they had stayed in Egypt—they had only come out to the wilderness to die. Moses, however, carried on trusting. Under Yahweh's instructions he urged the people on into the water. Suddenly a strong east wind began to blow. This drove the waters back. Now the people were able to cross the water, for it had become dry land. The Egyptians followed in hot pursuit. But at this point the wind turned again and the waters flowed back. The Egyptians sank into the soft sand as the waters quickly rose; they became stuck and bogged down by the wheels of their heavy chariots.

The sea of reeds

Read Exodus 14:10–31

According to tradition, the sea that the Israelites crossed (and the Egyptians sank into!) was the western arm of the Red Sea, an extremely deep and wide stretch of water that extends north-west from the southern tip of the Sinai peninsula. But that is not what the Hebrew Scriptures say! For according to Exodus the water that the Israelites crossed was called the 'Sea of Reeds'. You have to turn to the original Hebrew in which the Jewish Scriptures were written to discover that many English translations are not completely accurate here! Obviously therefore we should be looking for a kind of marshy sea or lake where reeds might grow. This *excludes* the Red Sea itself—because reeds don't and won't grow along its shores. But reeds do grow on the shores of several shallow marshy lakes that lie to the north of the Red Sea and just east of the land of Goshen. Today the Suez Canal passes through these lakes. It was probably at one of these comparatively small lakes that the crossing of the water occurred. If you look at the map of the route that the Israelites took, you can see that it is far more likely that they would need to cross

A mural depicting the Israelites crossing the sea safely while the Egyptian armies are drowned.

one of these lakes in their escape rather than the Red Sea itself, which was such a long way to the south.

After the crossing of the sea, the Israelites sang a song of rejoicing and praise to Yahweh. You can find two versions of the song given in Exodus: a short one, [**Exodus 15:21**] which Miriam sang, and the longer version [**Exodus 15:1–18**] sung by Moses and the people of Israel. Both versions of the song are very old. We can imagine that the Israelites would have remembered the song first sung on such an important occasion, and have sung it again and again in later years—whenever they had another victory to rejoice and sing about. This 'song of Moses' is poetry, and is very similar to many of the poems in the Psalms [see especially **Psalm 96 and 98**]. Notice how the crossing of the sea is described as a 'victory'—God is a warrior who has personally defeated the forces of Pharaoh. We ourselves would not think of God in quite these terms—perhaps because we have a long tradition of monotheism. In our view, God is so completely supreme that there is nothing and no-one for him to fight.

The significance of the 'sea'

Why is it important to find out which sea or lake the Bible is referring to? Well, obviously, if it was the deep waters of the Red Sea itself that the Israelites crossed, this was an event such as has never happened before or since. However, at the lakes further north a happening such as the Bible describes has been seen to take place at other times. Since the lakes are shallow and marshy, they do sometimes dry up when a strong wind blows from a particular direction. The miracle was that it happened precisely when it did! So if we are right, this means the crossing of the Sea of Reeds was a 'sign' very similar to the 'ten signs' that took place while the Israelites were in Egypt. Those, like Moses and the Israelites, who believed that Yahweh caused the wind to blow at exactly the right moment saw the correct 'significance' of what happened, but for Pharaoh and the Egyptians it was just a minor military disaster, not even 'significant' enough to record.

The Merneptah pillar

When did the departure from Egypt and the crossing of the sea take place? It is difficult to be absolutely sure, but if we put together evidence from both inside and outside the Hebrew

Statue of Merneptah, the Pharaoh who succeeded Rameses II. A stone pillar dating from Merneptah's reign helps us to work out when the Israelites left Egypt.

Scriptures, we can point to a date of about 1285 BC. Our reasons for thinking that this is the correct date are:

1. The departure from Egypt must have taken place sometime after the beginning of the reign of Rameses II, because the Israelites had been slave labourers building a city called Rameses after him. Pharaoh Rameses began to reign in 1290. However, his was an extremely long reign which lasted until 1225.

2. There is a stone pillar which comes from the time of the next pharaoh, Merneptah, that refers to Merneptah's victories in Canaan. Among those whom he defeated he lists Israel, 'Israel is no more, her seed is not.' The Merneptah pillar can be dated *precisely*—to the year 1220 BC.

This means that by 1220 the Israelites must have left Egypt, spent 'forty years' in the wilderness and established themselves in the land of Canaan. Even though the 'forty years' in the wilderness is not necessarily meant to be an exact period of time, but is rather a biblical expression meaning 'a long time', this would suggest that the departure of the Israelites from Egypt must have taken place at the beginning rather than the end of the reign of Rameses. So the date 1285 BC seems about right.

The Exodus

The name we generally give to the whole story of the ten signs, the Passover, the escape from Egypt and the crossing of the sea is the *Exodus*. It is in origin a Greek word and means 'departure'—the departure from Egypt. The Exodus was—and is—the most important event in Israel's life. We can even say that in a very real sense it 'created' Israel. Before the Exodus the Israelites were just an assortment of slaves who had no real sense of purpose and unity. They had forgotten that they came from a common family, and had a common ancestor. Instead the harsh conditions of their slavery led them to quarrel with each other [**Exodus 2:13**]. The Exodus made them into a people with a sense of unity. They were all one, for they were all Yahweh's people, the people of the God who had freed and saved them all.

Out of the land of Egypt: the Israelites never forgot the marvellous thing that happened at the Exodus. The memory of it influenced the way they viewed much of their later history.

The new Exodus

In the lives of some people there is an event that they remember above everything else. It has changed them so profoundly that it has become like a pair of spectacles through which they look at the rest of their lives. Nations can sometimes be like that as well. For the Israelites *the* event above all others was the Exodus. It was the event that had made them into a people to begin with, and it provided the set of spectacles through which they viewed their later history. So it is not surprising that, many centuries after the original Exodus had taken place, in one of their darkest moments the Israelites looked forward to a new Exodus to lead them to freedom once more.

In the year 586 BC Jerusalem was destroyed and many of the inhabitants were carried off into exile in Babylon. In the gloomy years of exile, while they were longing to return to Canaan, two great prophets spoke to the Israelites. They promised that, just as Yahweh had led his people across the desert from Egypt, so also he would lead them across the desert from Babylon. However, this new Exodus would be even more marvellous than the first, for it would not be a hurried escape, but a triumphal march [Isaiah 52:11–12].

Later still, the early Christian Church put on Exodus 'spectacles' to interpret the freedom from sin brought by Jesus Christ. But still today the Exodus theme which runs through the Bible is a powerful image. People who feel themselves oppressed and enslaved sometimes pray and hope for a new Exodus which will lead them to freedom and a promised land: the liberation of American slaves was compared to the Exodus.

9 You shall have no other gods before me

Yahweh looked after his people: he fed them with quails and (shown here) manna. (From a 12th century manuscript)

After the tremendous experience at the Sea of Reeds, Moses and the Israelites set off across the wilderness of Sinai. Assuming that the traditional site of Mount Sinai is correct, we can suggest that the Israelites would first have travelled in a southerly direction, keeping near to the coast. With such a large number of people travelling together, it was necessary to organise the journey on the basis of where water-holes and springs might be found. So the Israelites headed for Marah, where there was supposed to be water. But unexpectedly the water at Marah was brackish and bitter (the word Marah is a Hebrew word meaning 'bitter'), and so the people complained fiercely to Moses, who made the waters fresh and possible to drink. The situation was better at Elim, where they arrived next—here there was a sizeable oasis formed by twelve springs, and so the people encamped there for some time.

Murmuring and grumbling

The story of the complaints made by the Israelites at Marah is one example of a number of times during the wandering in the wilderness when the people are critical and impatient both with Yahweh and with Moses, his messenger. They complained about lack of water, about lack of food, about how much more comfortable life had been for them in Egypt! Again and again they seem to have doubted Yahweh's ability to help them, even though they had all experienced what he had done for them at the Sea of Reeds. Each time they grumbled, Yahweh came to their aid—making the bitter waters of Marah fresh **[Exodus 15:23]**, sending quails and manna for food **[Exodus 16:1–21]**, causing water to spring from a rock **[Exodus 17:6]**. Yahweh also came to their assistance when they had to fight a battle against the Amalekites, a

desert tribe who came and attacked the Israelites **[Exodus 17:8–13]**. It is easy to be wise after the event and feel that the Israelites ought to have had faith and trusted Yahweh, since they had already seen his power at work so forcefully. But we must remember three things:

1. Life in the desert is very uncertain when compared with life in a settled land such as Egypt. It was a great test of faith for the Israelites to move on, not knowing precisely where they were going nor how they would manage to find food and water for themselves and their animals. It is not surprising that sometimes they failed the test!

2. As we have already seen when thinking about the 'ten signs' and the crossing of the sea, God does not act in such a way that he compels faith. Biblical signs are not proofs that leave no room for doubts—people can choose whether to see them as Yahweh's mighty acts or just 'lucky' coincidences. God, in both the Old and the New Testament, respects people's free will. But this means that sometimes people will say 'no' rather than 'yes'.

3. It is remarkable that the Hebrew Scriptures are so honest about the number of times Israel complained and grumbled in the desert. All too often, both in ancient times and even today,

history is written as though it was a 'golden age' in which people were in every way better than they are in the present. By contrast, the Israelite account of the time in the desert is extremely honest—the people were not always saints or heroes, but all too ordinary human beings with all the usual faults.

Putting together these three points, we can say that a central theme of the Bible is the way in which God calls people to follow him in faith, but that over and over again people fail. In spite of that, God continues to love them and want them to turn to him again.

The covenant at Sinai

Read Exodus 19:10–25
After the Israelites left the springs at Elim to continue southwards, they would have come fairly quickly to an area which is known today as Serabit el-Khdam. This was an important mining centre for the Egyptians, where they dug for turquoise. The Israelites would have skirted the place, avoiding the Egyptian workmen as much as possible. After Serabit el-Khdam, the Israelites probably changed direction, and proceeded north-east, travelling along a gap in the mountains called the Wadi Firan (the Firan Valley). This would have brought them directly to Jebel Musa (Mount Sinai). There the Israelites camped opposite the mountain.

Jebel Musa is a rugged and forbidding place. The Israelites remembered what Moses had told them of his previous experience here—how it was here that he had first met Yahweh—and so they were terror-struck, afraid to approach the mountain too closely because of its 'holiness' (see section 6). So Moses went by himself up the mountain-side to meet with Yahweh. As he did so, he heard Yahweh addressing him, 'You saw what I, the LORD, did to the Egyptians and how I carried you as an eagle carries her young on her wings, and brought you here to me. Now, if you will obey me and keep my covenant, you will be my own people. The whole earth is mine, but you will be my chosen people, a people dedicated to me alone, and you will serve me as priests.' [Exodus 19:3–6].

Here we are at the heart of the message of

1. Worship no god but me.
2. Do not make for yourselves images.
3. Do not use my name for evil purposes.
4. Observe the Sabbath and keep it holy.
5. Respect your father and your mother.
6. Do not commit murder.
7. Do not commit adultery.
8. Do not steal.
9. Do not accuse anyone falsely.
10. Do not desire another man's wife, or anything else that he owns.

the Scriptures. Up to now God has shown his graciousness and his love by what he has done, in bringing the people out of Egypt and guiding them to this place. Now it is their turn as God asks them to respond to his love by making (and keeping) a covenant with him—a covenant to be his own special people. God's love calls forth humanity's response. Notice that the love of God always comes before the response that people are called to make, for it is central to the teaching of the Bible that the initiative always belongs to God.

What is the 'covenant' that God asks the people to make with him? We saw already in section 3 what a covenant was: a solemn agreement made on oath between two people or two groups of people. In the case of the covenant with Abraham, it was a covenant made between God and *one* man, but now at Sinai we have a covenant between God and a whole people. There are other differences too. In the covenant at Sinai God asks for a much greater degree of response from the people with whom he is making the covenant (remember how Abraham was actually asleep when God made a covenant with him!). Now the covenant depends not only on God's promise, but also on the willingness of the people to respond to his love by showing their willingness to keep his commandments.

The Ten Commandments

Read Exodus 20:1–17

There are ten commandments on which the covenant was based. They are technically called the Decalogue (which really means 'the ten words'). Ever since the time of Moses and Sinai, the Decalogue has been a foundation stone of the Israelite and Jewish religion. The Commandments are also very important for Christians, although Christians believe that they are best interpreted through the life and teachings of Jesus Christ.

The commandments are introduced by a reference to Yahweh and what he has done for the people, 'I am Yahweh your God who brought you out of the land of Egypt, where you were slaves' **[Exodus 20:2]**. The first commandment then immediately goes on to state that, because Yahweh has done this, the Israelites are to worship him alone. To worship any other god would be disloyal and ungrateful! Notice that the commandment is about not *worshipping* other gods. At this early stage in their history the Israelites probably did not believe that their God was the *only* God—they knew that there were other gods who were worshipped by other peoples and nations such as the Egyptians, but as far as the Israelites were concerned that was not important. What was important was that *they*, the Israelites, were not to worship these gods—they were only to worship God, the God who had chosen them for his own.

The second commandment prohibited the making of 'graven images'. In the world in which the Israelites lived it was the usual practice to make small and large statues of gods. Many such statues have been found by archaeologists in the Middle East. But the Israelites were expressly forbidden to make such images and statues. The first commandment had already prohibited the worship of any other god, so it must be statues of Yahweh himself that the second commandment was referring to. What was the reason for this? It was surely bound up with the purpose for which people made statues of their gods—they did so because then they believed that then they could 'capture' the god through his statue and make him work for them as they wanted. It was a form of

By making and worshipping an image of a golden calf, the Israelites were breaking the commandment which required them to worship only Yahweh, and the commandment which forbade the making of 'graven images'.

magic. But the second commandment says firmly that the religion of Israel was not to be like this. Yahweh was not a 'puppet' to be manipulated as people wanted. Instead he was a god who had to be free to act as his holy nature demanded.

The third commandment was very similar to the second—'Do not use my name for evil purposes.' Just as making a statue of a person or a god was felt to be a way of gaining control over them, so also, knowing a person's name gave power. Yahweh took a big risk when he revealed his name to the Israelites—so now he prohibits its misuse. The Israelites may not use it in any magical way to command Yahweh to do precisely what they want.

The commandment about the keeping of the sabbath day was an important way of affirming Yahweh's lordship over his people. He had given them everything—freedom, and eventually land and peoplehood. To keep the sabbath day as a special day 'for Yahweh' was a symbolic way in which the Israelites could recognise how much they owed to Yahweh, and perhaps give him something of themselves in return.

The other six commandments concerned the Israelites themselves, and the ways they behaved to each other. But they are based on the prior assumption that the Israelites are meant to be *one* people, because they are Yahweh's people—so Yahweh himself is concerned if there is disunity and trouble among the Israelites. So the final six commandments set limits: it is impossible for the Israelites to be Yahweh's people if there is stealing, murder, adultery and false witness among them. These six commandments are not meant to be a complete law-code for Israelite society, and so there are many aspects of life they do not touch upon. What they attempt to do is to set the limits of completely unacceptable behaviour—there is no way a person who breaks one of these fundamental commandments can fit into the community of Israel, the people of Yahweh. Most of these six 'social' commandments are easy to understand. Perhaps the last commandment is rather more difficult. The people are ordered not to desire, or covet, each other's property. The word 'covet' used in many versions of the Bible means something much stronger than being jealous or envious of other people's talents or possessions. In the context of the Ten Commandments it refers to being so jealous or envious of other people's possessions that you take steps to seize them for yourself.

The golden calf

Read Exodus 32:1–9

The Hebrew Scriptures are always extremely realistic about the Israelites. One would have imagined that, while the people were still at Mount Sinai, just after they had made their covenant with Yahweh, it ought to have been possible for them to manage to keep the commandments. But no. Almost straight away they broke both the first and second commandments by making and worshipping a golden calf. What made it worse was that Aaron, Moses' brother, was weak enough to permit this to happen while Moses was still on the mountain talking with Yahweh. People and priest were both guilty. The forgiveness of Yahweh was needed, as it was to be needed many times in later history.

A good example of what the Hebrew Scriptures mean by 'covet' occurs in 1 Kings 21. King Ahab and Queen Jezebel want a particular vineyard so badly that they put its owner, Naboth, to death. Breaking the tenth commandment led Ahab to break the sixth, eighth and ninth commandments as well!

The Ark of the Covenant

What had delayed Moses on the mountain was a conversation in which he received the blueprint for a box that was to accompany the Israelites on their future journeys. This box, called an 'Ark', was to contain the tablets on which were written the Ten Commandments of the covenant. The Israelites would at least never be able to say that they did not know what the commandments were! We hear of the Ark from time to time in the later history of Israel. Because of its connection with the covenant at Sinai, it is often called the Ark of the Covenant. The Ark, however, had another even more important significance. In some mysterious way the presence of Yahweh himself was bound up with the Ark. As the Ark journeyed with the Israelites in the wilderness and later into the land of Canaan, it was a symbol that Yahweh was travelling with his people wherever they went. They had not left him behind at Mount Sinai!

10 Into the land of Canaan

Overcoming the setbacks

Moses himself was not to enter the land of Canaan. Standing on Mount Nebo, a mountain lying five miles east of the River Jordan, he would have glimpsed the land which had been his goal for so many years, but he died before the Jordan could be crossed. He had not had an easy time as leader of the Israelites. He had attempted first of all to enter Canaan from the south, coming from Sinai up to the oasis of Kadesh-Barnea, and then pushing northwards into Canaan. But this had proved disastrous. The Israelites had been met by the Amalekites, a desert tribe whose stronghold seems to have been in the south of Canaan, and had been completely routed in the battle that followed [**Numbers 14:39–45**]. It then took several years to recover their strength after the catastrophe.

Realising that the Amalekites seemed to present an insuperable barrier to entering Canaan directly from the south, Moses then turned towards the east. He intended to lead the Israelites across the Negev desert until they were south-east of the Dead Sea and then turn north, through Edom and Moab, and finally, once they were north of the Dead Sea, take them across the River Jordan which marked the eastern boundary of the land of Canaan. But even this diversion did not work out quite according to plan. Not surprisingly, the Kings of Edom and Moab were suspicious of the intentions of this large group of people that were wanting to travel through their territory. So they forbade the Israelites to use the route running from south to north through Edom and Moab. Instead, the Israelites had to go even further east and by-pass the two countries. This meant a longer journey, and one that was not so well provided with watering places for their herds and flocks.

Eventually the Israelites reached the Jordan. On Moses' death, Joshua, a young man that he had been training for several years, took over as leader of the people. The Jordan was crossed without any problem. We do not have to believe that the Jordan literally stopped flowing. Nowhere is it a wide river, and at the point where the Israelites would have crossed it, just north of where it flows into the Dead Sea, it is really quite shallow, having lost a lot of water through evaporation. During much of the year it is still possible to ford the Jordan at this point. As the Israelites crossed the Jordan, they remembered how they, or perhaps their fathers, had 40 years before crossed the Sea of Reeds. In their minds the two 'crossings' were linked, for the ultimate goal of the freedom that had been won by the crossing of the Sea of Reeds was the gift of the land of Canaan, foreshadowed by the crossing of the Jordan.

The walls of Jericho

Read Joshua 6
Once across the Jordan, the first major city Joshua and the Israelites reached was Jericho.

Joshua led the Israelites across the Jordan, which was shallow enough for them to ford.

Jericho and archaeology

There are some problems connected with Joshua's capture of Jericho that we must consider briefly. One problem is bound up with archaeology. The site of ancient Jericho has been 'dug' by archaeologists several times, most recently by the British archaeologist Kathleen Kenyon between 1951 and 1958. But though Kathleen Kenyon discovered much of great interest in her 'dig' at Jericho, including a stone tower that is perhaps 11 000 years old, she did not find any important remains that seemed to come from the time of Joshua, nor from several centuries before. She felt that it was doubtful whether Jericho was inhabited at the time of Joshua. Obviously if this is so, there is a conflict between what the Bible says and the findings of archaeology. What are we to make of this?

We ought to remember that archaeologists can and do make mistakes. Sometimes an archaeologist digs at a site, believing it to be a particular ancient city, and it turns out to be quite another. It is also possible for archaeologists to make mistakes about the date of their finds, because archaeology is not an exact science and the interpretation of archaeological data is affected by the judgment of an individual archaeologist. However, these factors probably do not apply at Jericho. The mound that Kenyon dug was almost certainly Jericho, and equally she was undoubtedly correct when she stated that no important remains on the site came from the time of Joshua. The answer may be that at Jericho the sandy soil and the extreme climate in the area meant that there has been a great deal of erosion. Perhaps, quite literally, the city of the time of Joshua was washed away from the top of the mound!

This lies only a mile to the west of the river. It was an important town at that time, and effectively controlled the passes which led up into the hills to the west. It was therefore a necessity for the Israelites to capture Jericho if they wanted to be able to move up into the hill country and more fertile parts of Canaan.

The capture of Jericho is related in the Book of Joshua. It is a vivid and exciting account, well worth reading. Perhaps the Israelites retold the story of the capture of Jericho from time to time, maybe even acting it out with the help of trumpets. They believed God himself had fought for them; it was not they themselves but Yahweh who had won the victory. **Joshua 5:13–15** makes this clear.

A pair of stained-glass windows from Lincoln Cathedral. From left: Joshua carrying the Ark of the Covenant; meeting the 'man with the sword', who was the angelic captain of

Yahweh's army—thus Joshua's victory was really Yahweh's; capture of Jericho, the 'gateway' to Canaan, which the Israelites had to take before they moved west.

Moving on

After the capture of Jericho the Israelites moved westwards. As they did so they would have had to climb sharply up into the hill country. Jericho is 250 metres *below* sea level, while Ai, the next city they hoped to reach, is about 750 metres *above* sea level. To reach Ai they would have travelled along one of the dry river beds, or wadis, that run down from the hill country to the plain of the Jordan. Throughout history this is the way many invading armies have come, since it is the easiest way to reach the central plateau on which Jerusalem and many of the other major cities of the country are located.

Holy war

Read Joshua 7
At first the Israelite attempt to capture Ai was unsuccessful, and some of the Israelites were killed. Joshua investigated and he discovered that this had happened because one of the Israelites, called Achan, had broken God's command. After the capture of Jericho he had kept for himself some gold trophies that he had seized as spoil in the city. This gives us a new insight into the kind of war that the Israelites were fighting. It was a 'holy war'. It was Yahweh's war they believed they were fighting as they tried to conquer the land, and so they felt that Yahweh himself was fighting with them and on their behalf. This meant that the spoil and booty taken in the war belonged to Yahweh and was not to be kept by the Israelites themselves. They had to dedicate it to God and sacrifice it in a gigantic fire at the end of the day's victory. Achan had broken these rules and brought down Yahweh's anger upon his own head and upon his people. His punishment was dramatic and swift: he, his family and all his possessions were stoned and burned by the rest of the Israelites. Perhaps that helps put in perspective things such as the slaughter of the people of Jericho which we find difficult to understand and impossible to justify—the Israelites were prepared to be just as ruthless to their fellow countrymen if the occasion called for it, as they were to the enemies they defeated in battle.

The division of the land

Read Judges 1:27–36
After Achan's death the Israelites did manage to capture Ai. According to **Joshua 11:23**, Joshua went on from there to take the whole land, and then divided it among the tribes. But we need to look very closely at the Bible here. For if you read the beginning of Judges [**Judges 1:27–36**], you find it quite clearly stated that the Israelites did not capture all the land of Canaan at the time of Joshua. The passages give us a list of all the areas where the Canaanites remained in control even after the coming of the Israelites into the land, and this list includes many of the most important cities of Canaan.

What are we to make of this difference between Judges and Joshua? Most probably the picture given us by **Judges 1** is more realistic than the impression given by **Joshua 11:23**. It is quite likely that for a considerable period of time after the Israelites first came into the land—perhaps right up to the time of David—there were many areas of Canaan where the

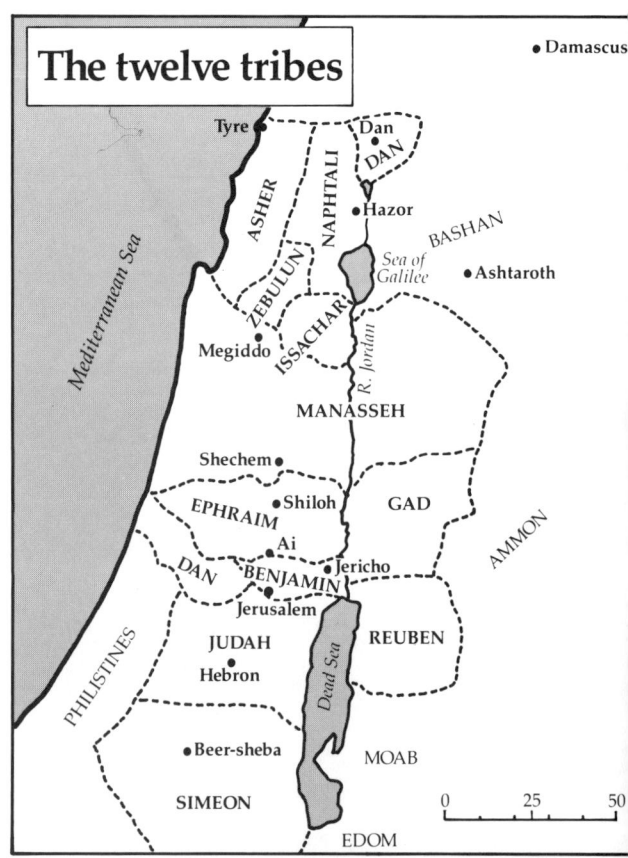

The twelve tribes

The Gibeonites made a treaty with the Israelites—though trickery was involved. Read Joshua 9.

Canaanites rather than the Israelites were in control. Because of this, many people wonder whether we should really talk of a 'conquest' of the land by the Israelites at the time of Joshua. They wonder whether it might be more accurate to speak of a 'settlement'. They would suggest that, though the Israelites under Joshua might immediately have captured some cities such as Jericho and Ai, the process was really much more gradual.

The covenant at Shechem

Read Joshua 24:1–28
Sometimes the Israelites succeeded in making a treaty and came to terms with the inhabitants of a particular town. They seem to have done this in the case of the Gibeonites. However, in other parts of the country the Canaanite cities were altogether too strong for the Israelites. When this happened, the Israelites who wanted to settle in the area had a choice of two options. Either they could try and live a semi-settled life on the hillsides, at some distance from the city, or they could, and sometimes did, offer their services as slave labourers to the Canaanites.

The situation at Shechem was different yet again. At this city, in the central part of the land of Canaan, Israelite men and Canaanite women married each other. The Israelites got the right to live in the city because of their Canaanite wives. After the campaign to take Jericho and Ai, Shechem, perhaps because of its location, gradually became a base for the Israelites. After some years in the land, Joshua gathered all the tribes to Shechem. They re-affirmed the original covenant they had made with God at Sinai. At the same time some other groups of people, perhaps distant kinsmen of the Israelites, who had not been in Egypt or at Sinai, expressed their desire to join with the Israelites. Joshua was happy to allow them to do this. The condition was that they put away other gods and worshipped only Yahweh. New Israelites and old gathered together before a great stone at Shechem and pledged their loyalty and obedience.

The Book of the Covenant

Laws were very important in ancient Israel. At Sinai, the relationship God had established with Israelites had been based upon the Ten Commandments. If their covenant with Yahweh was to continue, then the people had to keep these laws. Gradually, however, other laws began also to be observed by the Israelites. One group of such laws can be found in **Exodus 21–23:19**. They are sometimes referred to as 'the Book of the Covenant'. We know that the laws of the Book of the Covenant, though old, do not quite go back to the time of Moses and the covenant at Sinai. This is because several of them deal with the situation of a farming people in a settled land. They would not have made any sense to the Israelites when they were wandering in the desert. Probably the laws of the Book of the Covenant come from the time of Joshua and the settlement in the land of Canaan. The Book of the Covenant was therefore very significant in the life of ancient Israel, but it was not so absolutely central to their relationship with Yahweh as were the Ten Commandments. All the same, the laws in the Book of the Covenant are important. Many of them are concerned with the poor, and with ensuring that the weaker members of society, such as widows and orphans, are not oppressed by those in power. If we compare the Book of the Covenant with other lawcodes in the ancient world, such as the Babylonian Code of Hammurabi, we can see how exceptional this concern is.

11   The religion of Canaan

Once the Israelites had entered the land of Canaan, almost inevitably they began to be influenced by the culture of the people who already lived in the land. Gradually they began to grow crops, such as wheat and barley, and they also kept animals. Their lifestyle became that of settled farmers rather than nomadic shepherds. They learnt about trade and about working metals. One important part of the life of the Canaanites was their religion: they were polytheists, worshipping several gods, although their most important god was probably Baal. From almost the very first moment that the Israelites arrived in Canaan, they were fascinated by and attracted to the worship of Baal. Time and time again Judges tells us that the Israelites, 'did what was evil in the sight of Yahweh and served Baal'. What was it about the worship of Baal that made it such a temptation to the Israelites?

The Ugaritic tablets

Since 1929 we know a great deal about the worship of Baal and the other gods of the Canaanites. In that year a farmer ploughing his fields at a place known today as Ras Shamra in north Syria came across some ancient ruins. Archaeologists were called in and found not only the remains of an important city—ancient Ugarit—but also a large collection of tablets. These tablets were written in cuneiform script but, unlike in Mesopotamian cuneiform (see section 2), the cuneiform characters of the Ugaritic tablets each represent *one* letter rather than a whole syllable. This means that there were comparatively few characters to learn— only 30—and so it has been quite easy for scholars to read the Ugaritic texts and find out what they say. Some of the texts tell us about the history of Ugarit itself. We hear that it was an important town, trading in bronze and copper with the island of Cyprus, that it was ruled by a series of kings, and that it was destroyed by

Parched earth south of the Dead Sea: one reason why some Israelites were tempted to worship Baal the Thunderer (above), the most important Canaanite god.

enemies in about 1400 BC. After this time it never really recovered, and eventually all trace of it disappeared under the soil, until it was discovered earlier this century.

The gods of Ugarit

However, the most important texts from Ugarit tell us a great deal about the worship and religious beliefs of the people who lived in the city. They worshipped many gods, who were believed to live together in splendour on a high mountain, Mount Zaphon, which lies some miles north of Ugarit. Although these gods were officially under the rule of 'El', king of the gods, they seem to have been a very unruly lot and spent a great deal of time fighting each other!

Each of the gods had his own special interests. They liked to support these interests, often at the expense of other gods. For example El, king of the gods, is associated with the sky. He is depicted as an old man. He is married to a goddess called Asherah who has some connection with the sea. But although El is officially king, he does not seem to be as active or powerful as a younger god, Baal, who is the most important of the gods in the Ugaritic texts. Baal is the god who is concerned with the fertility of the land. He gives the rain that enables the crops to grow. So he is often called Baal-Hadad, 'Baal the Thunderer'. If you look at the picture of the statue of Baal you can see that he is shown with his hand raised, about to throw a bolt of lightning.

Baal is a warrior god, and in the stories from Ugarit he has two main enemies, the god Yamm, and the god Mot. Yamm is the god of the seas and the unruly waters, all the chaotic forces that threaten to drown the crops growing in the land. Since these crops are Baal's special concern, he fights Yamm and, although the contest is fierce, Baal eventually defeats him completely. Mot, however, proves a more dangerous enemy. His name means 'Death' and he is the god associated with the forces of heat and drought that cause all the vegetation of Canaan to wither and die every summer. Mot fights Baal, and this time Baal seems to be the loser. He dies and goes down to the underworld. But the story is not yet over, for after some months Baal comes to life again, fights Mot once more, but this time manages to defeat him.

The gods of the seasons

What is important to realise about the gods of ancient Ugarit is that they are really very little more than personifications of the climate and the seasons of Canaan. Baal was the personification of the healthily growing crops that were planted each autumn. They needed his rains to make them grow, but at the same time it was important that there were no floods to wash away the young plants, so Yamm had to be defeated. Mot is the personification of the summer, the dry period of the year. The wheat and barley have now been harvested, and any plants left behind wither in the fierce summer heat. The ground becomes hard and arid. There is no rain between May and October. And so Baal 'dies'—that is only to be expected. But it is important that he should come to life again in the autumn, to bring the rains once more and ensure that the crops for the next year could be planted and begin to grow. So we can see that the religion of the people of Ugarit was completely tied up with their agricultural way of life and with ensuring that it was successful.

The rain from heaven

For the Canaanite farmer, the rainfall difference between Jerusalem and Jericho meant in practical terms that, if he lived near Jerusalem or to the west, he could grow his crops of wheat and barley. But 10 km to the east of the city, where the rainfall is less than 300 mm each year, there is no possibility of harvesting grain, of growing olives and fig trees. And only 13–15 km from Jerusalem he was in the desert, where virtually nothing would grow.

The desert—and the people who might come from it to try and steal his land—were an ever-present threat to the Canaanite farmer. Sometimes the desert might even begin to encroach upon his lands. For although 660 mm is the average annual rainfall in Jerusalem, there are many years when the rainfall may be less than this. In these years the farmer would watch the desert begin to creep nearer, and if there was a succession of years with poor rainfall, the desert might even engulf his lands. If that happened, there would

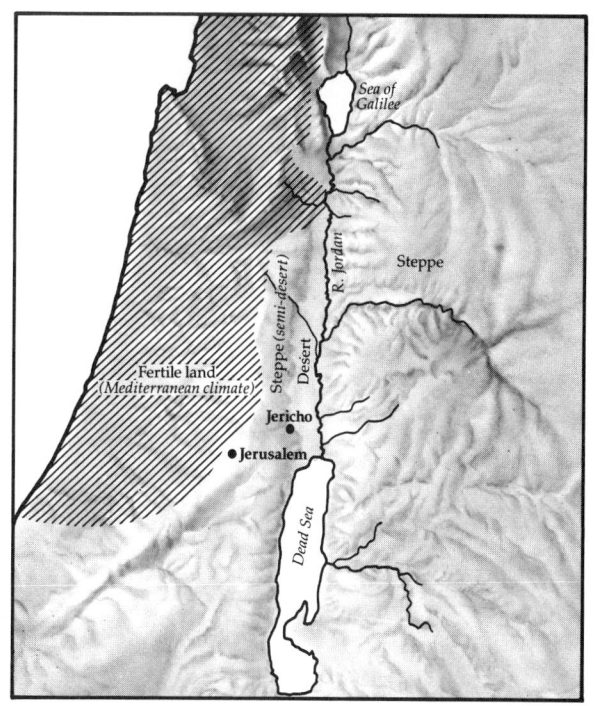

be famine. No wonder the Canaanite farmer prayed very hard for rain! (See page 8.)

The temptation to worship Baal

The Canaanites whom the Israelites met when they came into the land had similar religious beliefs and practices to the people of Ugarit. And we can see just why they would have seemed so attractive to the Israelites. For as the Israelites began to live the life of settled farmers, the seasons of the year, the time of rain and the time of drought became very important to them. To many Israelites it was only logical to worship Baal to ensure rain for their crops. Yahweh was a god whom they had met in the desert. 'Surely', they probably said to themselves, 'Yahweh is a god of the desert, and he has no experience in making our crops grow here in the fertile land. For this we need to worship Baal—after all, that is what the people who have lived here for centuries do. It is only natural that, now we have come to live among them and share their way of life, we ought to worship Baal too. We won't stop worshipping Yahweh, but we really don't see why we can't worship both Yahweh and Baal.' That was the dilemma that confronted the Israelites when they arrived in Canaan. It was a dilemma that remained with them for many hundreds of years, in fact until 586 BC when Jerusalem was destroyed and the people exiled to Babylon. Many Israelites were completely disloyal to Yahweh, and others tried to worship Baal and Yahweh at the same time. It was the work of prophets like Elijah, who lived in the ninth century BC, to tell the people that it was impossible to worship both Baal and Yahweh [**1 Kings 18:21**].

The agricultural festivals

Read Exodus 23:14–17
One aspect of agricultural life in Canaan that the Israelites could not avoid encountering was the harvest festivals that took place several times in the year. There were three major festivals in the Canaanite agricultural year. The most important was the Feast of Ingathering which took place at the end of September or the beginning of October. This is when the gathering of the grapes, figs and olives is completed, the dry heat of summer is drawing to a close, and people are looking forward eagerly

Would there be a good harvest this year? It all depended on the rain—and still does in the Middle East today.

to the coming of the autumn rains in late October. At the Feast of Ingathering people gave thanks to the gods for the harvest they had recently gathered. At the same time they prayed for the prosperity of the coming year as they waited for the rain.

The second festival was the Feast of Unleavened Bread. This took place in March or April at the beginning of the barley harvest.

About fifty days after the Feast of Unleavened Bread came the third feast of the year. This was the Feast of Weeks. It commemorated the end of the wheat harvest.

We know that these Canaanite agricultural festivals were adopted by the Israelites. There are many references to them in the Hebrew Scriptures [**Exodus 23:14–17**]. However, although the Israelites adopted the feasts, they changed them in important ways. For one thing, it was Yahweh that they were commanded to thank for the good harvests they had just enjoyed—not Baal. But, in addition, they did not just thank Yahweh for the blessings of that year's harvest. At the same time they also thanked him for what he had done for them throughout their history as a people. We can see this very clearly in **Deuteronomy 26:1–11**.

Religious festivals

Gradually, as the years passed, the Israelites began to link particular parts of their history with particular festivals. At the Feast of Unleavened Bread they remembered the slavery in Egypt, and Yahweh's miraculous leading of his people in the Exodus towards freedom. Since they had previously celebrated a nomadic festival, the Passover, at this time of year (see section 7), eventually they drew together the Feast of Unleavened Bread and the celebration of Passover and started to treat them as two parts of the same festival.

At the Feast of Weeks the Israelites especially remembered the giving of the law and the covenant at Sinai. The Feast of Ingathering was eventually given a new name by the Israelites. They called it the Feast of Tabernacles or Booths. In September each year the villagers of Canaan would go to their vineyards outside the villages and towns and live in temporary huts or 'booths' that they made there while they gathered their grapes. This custom reminded the Israelites of the temporary dwellings and tents they had used in the wilderness after the escape from Egypt. So the particular theme re-

membered at the Feast of Ingathering or Booths became the wandering in the wilderness.

Just as the Israelites took over and gave new meanings to feasts that had originally belonged to other religions, so also, in the past, Christianity has 'adopted' festivals and rites that were originally pagan. The best example of this is perhaps the keeping of Christmas—the Christian Church in the fourth century AD 'took over' a pagan festival which honoured the sun towards the end of December each year and used it to remember the birth of Christ, 'the Sun of Righteousness'.

The Gezer Calendar

Why does our year begin in January? Partly, at least, because it is then that the days begin to lengthen again after the short days at the end of December. Light is important to us. The way in which a people think about time always reveals their priorities.

At the beginning of this century a small piece of stone with Hebrew writing on it was discovered. It is a kind of calendar, called the Gezer Calendar after the place where it was found. It describes the farmer's year in ancient Canaan:

Two months of olive harvest
Two months of sowing
Two months of late planting
One month of hoeing the flax
One month of reaping barley
One month of harvest and feasting
Two months of vine-tending
One month of summer fruit

The Gezer Calendar is an important source of information about the agricultural year. Notice how it begins with the two months of olive harvest, which occurred in September/October. This was the most important time of year for the Canaanites and the Israelites, because it was then that the dry summer was drawing to a close and people were eagerly awaiting the rain.

12 In the days of the judges

After the covenant at Shechem and the death of Joshua, the Israelites were led by a series of rulers whom the Hebrew Scriptures call 'judges'. Though they probably did have the responsibility of deciding cases and arguments that arose between individual Israelites, the word 'judge' is not really very helpful, since their job was not restricted to legal matters. Perhaps 'chieftain' or 'ruler' gives a better idea of the task of the judges. Some judges, such as Samson, seem to have been very far removed from our picture of a judge. Samson's chief role was as a leader in war.

The twelve tribes

Israelite society in the days of the judges was not highly organised. Each Israelite family belonged to a tribe, and there were twelve of these, although the tribe of Joseph, the biggest of all the tribes, was early on divided into two sub-tribes, Ephraim and Manasseh. Probably tribal loyalty was much more intense than loyalty to 'Israel' as a whole. People thought of themselves as 'Danites' or 'Benjaminites' before they thought of themselves as Israelites. We can find out some interesting details about the tribes in two tribal lists that come at the end of Genesis and Deuteronomy. First Jacob blesses his twelve sons, the ancestors of the twelve tribes [Genesis 49:1–27]. Later on, after the Exodus, Moses himself blesses the twelve tribes just before his death [Deuteronomy 33]. From these blessings we can discover, for example, that the tribe of Zebulun lived by the sea [Genesis 49:13], that the tribe of Levi was a priestly tribe [Deuteronomy 33:8–10], that many of the tribe of Issachar had been compelled to turn themselves into slave-labourers [Genesis 49:14–15].

The Song of Deborah

Read Judges 5

The Song of Deborah is another source of information about the history of the twelve tribes. This Song may well be one of the oldest parts of the Hebrew Scriptures to be actually written down. Much of the history of the Israelites that we have studied so far was remembered and told orally for several generations before being put down in writing, but the Song of Deborah seems to have been written down almost as soon as Deborah finished singing it!

The Song tells of a victory that the Israelite tribes had over the Canaanite Jabin, King of Hazor, a big city of Galilee, and over Sisera, the commander of Jabin's army. Interestingly enough, the leader of the Israelites at this time was a woman, Deborah, who is described as

The Israelites could not compete with Canaanite chariots.

Mount Tabor, the site of Deborah's famous victory.

being both a prophet and a judge. Deborah herself does not take part in the fighting—but she definitely gives the orders to Barak, who acts as the general of the Israelite army. The victory is a dramatic one—the Israelites mustered their troops on Mount Tabor, above the Canaanites in the plain below. Suddenly the Kishon river, which flows at the foot of Tabor, burst its banks. The Canaanites who were in their battle-chariots found themselves bogged down in the mud and water of the overflowing river. As they tried to make their escape on foot, the waiting Israelites fell upon them and devastated them in the confusion. Sisera, the Canaanite commander, managed to flee from the battlefield. Little good did it do him! He tried to hide in the tent of Haber the Kenite, whom he had thought to be an ally. But Heber's wife, Jael, was a friend of Deborah and, while Sisera was asleep, she killed him with a tent-peg. The ultimate insult of those days—he was slain by a woman!

However, not all the Israelites were involved in the victory over Jabin and Sisera. The Song of Deborah makes that clear. For Deborah, even while she celebrates the great victory, complains that some of the tribes had not bothered to turn up and fight. The tribe of Gad had stayed in its own territory east of the Jordan. Asher and Dan had both remained down by the sea instead of responding to Deborah's summons to all Israel to come to the assistance of those Israelites who had been threatened by the King of Hazor. And there were some tribes, such as Judah, who are not even mentioned in the Song—they didn't turn up to join in the fight, but they don't get a rebuke from Deborah.

The Israelite federation

So the Song of Deborah has made people wonder just how far the twelve tribes of Israel worked together in the days of the judges. And the answer seems to be, 'not very much'. What the tribes did have in common was their shared religious faith in Yahweh. They expressed this common faith in a variety of ways. It is likely that at least once each year the tribes gathered together to celebrate a religious festival. This may have been in origin an agricultural festival at the season of harvest (see section 11), but at the same time they remembered the covenant they had made with God at Sinai. Each year they 'renewed' this covenant and promised to continue to keep the Ten Commandments. On the same occasion they took the opportunity to settle disputes that had arisen between the different tribes. It was here that the 'judges' had an important role to play.

Where did the tribes meet? Probably at the place where the Ark of the Covenant was kept. In the early days of the judges this seems to have been at Shechem, but later on the Ark of the Covenant was moved to Shiloh. We might call this loose system of government a 'federation'.

After the tribes had returned home, it was then the responsibility of the judge to call them together again if one of the tribes was threatened by an external enemy—such as Jabin of Hazor. The judge would summon all the tribes to come and fight a 'holy war' for Yahweh, because Yahweh himself was threatened whenever his people were under threat. We have already seen, though, that the judges were not always completely successful in getting all possible support. As at the time of Deborah, generally only those tribes most closely affected by the 'enemy' came to fight with any great enthusiasm.

51

Gideon and the Midianites

Read Judges 7:1–23

Sometimes the judge himself led the people into battle. Gideon did so when the Israelites were under threat from the Midianites. The Midianites came from the east, from the desert—as had the Israelites a hundred years before. But these Midianites came not to stay, but to raid the fields on their swift camels and then retreat once more to the desert. In fact, they made use of camels to a far greater extent than anyone had done before. It made them a powerful and dangerous enemy. And so the fields of the Israelites were soon bare—the people began to suffer from famine.

Gideon was called by Yahweh to be the leader the Israelites needed. Gathering a select group of men, he tested them and weeded out the doubtful and hesitant. He did this by taking them down to the spring of Ein Harod and watching how the men drank. Then he divided them up into two groups. In the one group he put the men who lapped the water as a dog does, in the other those who knelt down and sensibly cupped the water with their hands. Surprisingly, it was the group who lapped that he chose to come with him—for in lapping the water as they did they had shown themselves oblivious to danger and prepared to trust Yahweh to the uttermost.

Gideon was left with only 300 men, but that was enough. This war with the Midianites was to be a 'holy war' in which Yahweh would be fighting on his people's behalf. The victory was swift. Gideon and the 300 men hid outside the camp of the Midianites. In the middle of the night, when the watchmen were drowsy, they smashed large numbers of pottery jars and blew loudly on trumpets. In the noise and confusion they fell upon the Midianites, who stood absolutely no chance against them. Many were slaughtered on the spot—those that managed to escape were pursued by the Israelites and cornered by them at the fords of the Jordan.

It was a convincing victory, and the grateful Israelites wanted to make Gideon king over them. But he refused. He said it was not *he* but rather God who should be their king. Gideon believed that, when the Israelites had made a covenant with God at Sinai, in doing so they had really agreed to be Yahweh's people and to accept Yahweh *alone* as their king. Gideon was only reminding the Israelites of this.

Abimelech, the thistle king

Read Judges 9:7–14

Unfortunately, Abimelech, Gideon's son, did not see matters quite like this. He was Gideon's son by a Canaanite woman, born in Shechem, and he had grown up in the Canaanite culture in which having a king was expected and normal. After Gideon's death he made himself king at Shechem over both Canaanites and Israelites. In the process he killed all his brothers except for one, Jotham, who managed to escape and hide. Jotham predicted that Abimelech's kingship would be a disaster. He said that it would be like a thistle trying to rule over the trees, even the lofty and majestic cedar.

Within three years, Jotham was proved right. The people of Shechem fell out with Abimelech—his retaliation was brutal. He set fire to a building in which many of them had gathered, and about a thousand people perished in the flames. But Abimelech himself was shortly to meet his end. While he was besieging another town, Thebez, one of the defenders, a woman,

The death of Abimelech. He was *not* a good advertisement for the idea of having a king!

Though blinded by his Philistine captors, Samson scored a final victory in his death.

managed to heave a millstone down upon his head and crush his skull. So died Abimelech, and with him the first attempt by the Israelites to have a human king. It had not been very successful! Not surprisingly when, some time in the future, the Israelites thought once more about having a king, many people remembered what a disaster Abimelech had been and were not at all happy with the idea.

The period of the judges was a turbulent time in Israelite history. There were several other judges whom we have not mentioned here, although we will refer to Samson the judge in more detail in section 13. About many judges we know little more than that they judged Israel for a number of years.

One constant theme that runs through Judges is the extent to which the Israelites turned from Yahweh to worship the Baals. The harsh refrain comes again and again, 'And the people of Israel again did what was evil in the sight of the Lord and served the Baals . . .' As the prophet Hosea was to put it many years later: Israel's love for Yahweh was like the morning dew that evaporated all too quickly at the slightest test.

13 The Philistines, people of the sea

Who were the Philistines?

Towards the end of the period of the judges we begin to hear a good deal about a new enemy that threatened the Israelites. They presented a far greater danger than any opposition the Israelites had encountered before. These people did not come from the desert. Instead and unusually they came from the west, from the sea. In the Hebrew Scriptures they are called the 'Philistines', but the Egyptians and the Canaanites called them 'the Peoples of the Sea'.

Who were the Philistines and where did they come from to give such trouble to the Israelites? Much later on in the Hebrew Scriptures the prophet Amos, talking about Yahweh being in control of all the nations of the world, says to Yahweh, 'Did you not bring the Philistines from Caphtor?' [Amos 9:7]. So where then is Caphtor? Most likely Caphtor is the island which today we call Crete, one of the Greek islands in the south Aegean Sea. What had caused the Philistines to leave Crete and come to look for a new home in Canaan?

The Minotaur, half-bull and half-man, was a fearsome creature in a Cretan legend.

From Crete to Canaan

The civilisation of Crete is one of the oldest cultures in the world. The archaeologists who unearthed the ruins of the capital of Crete at Knossos were amazed at the level of sophistication they discovered. The Cretans were 'ancient' even to the people *we* call the ancient Greeks, the inhabitants of Athens in the fourth and fifth centuries BC. The Athenians told stories and legends about the people of Crete, of their fabulous wealth, their royal palaces, their cities and even a labyrinth in which a strange monster called the Minotaur was kept.

The Athenians also told stories about the end of the great civilisation on Crete. The end had come when the land of Atlantis near Crete had suddenly sunk beneath the waves of the sea. For many years these tales told by the ancient Athenians were regarded as fiction without any basis in fact. But at the beginning of this century Knossos was excavated and it was possible to see that the Athenians were right when they talked about the great riches of the Cretans.

More recently, the truth behind that strange

Knossos: the Verandah of the Royal Guard. The city of Knossos was the capital of ancient Crete.

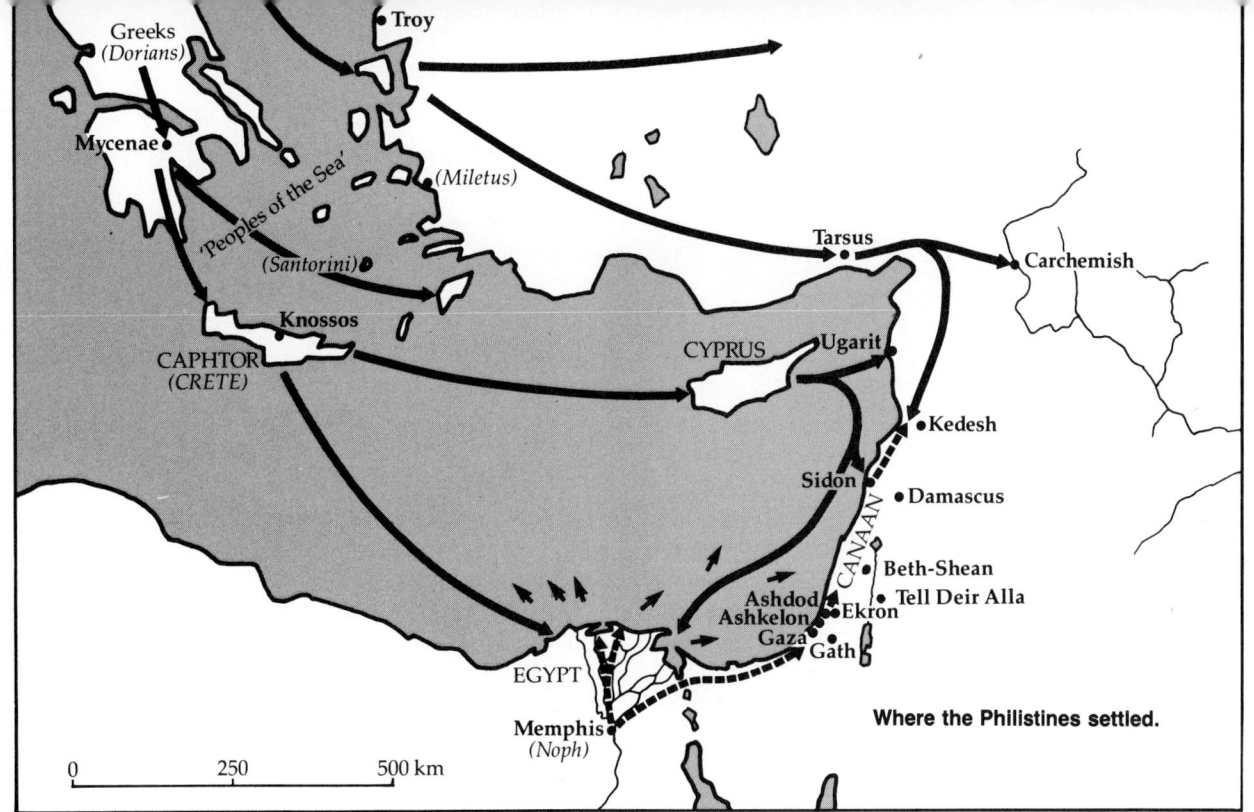

Where the Philistines settled.

account of the sinking of Atlantis has come to light. For not far from Crete there is an island called Santorini. The extremely strange shape of Santorini can be explained because it is part of the crater of an extinct volcano. In recent years studies have indicated that there was a massive volcanic eruption on Santorini about 1200 BC. This eruption was far bigger than any volcanic eruption that has been experienced in modern history. It blew up and destroyed most of the island of Santorini. It also set off enormous tidal waves which hit nearby islands such as Crete. Such powerful waves would have overwhelmed the coastal towns and cities of Crete, and dealt a savage blow to civilisation on the island. This was the origin of the story of Atlantis.

The consequences of the eruption also led the Philistines to leave Crete in search of a new home. First of all they tried to settle in Egypt. They sailed to the delta of the Nile. However, as Egyptian records tell us, the Pharaohs were powerful enough to fight off these 'Peoples of the Sea' and prevent them from establishing themselves in Egypt. All the same, the Egyptians had to come to terms. They agreed to let the Philistines settle along the coast of Canaan, which was then officially under Egyptian influence. They even allowed the Philistines to act as kind of 'policemen' in Canaan, overseeing the situation on behalf of the Egyptians.

The five cities of the Philistines

Read 1 Samuel 13:19–22

So the Philistines established themselves in five cities in the south of Canaan: Gaza, Gath, Ashdod, Ashkelon and Ekron. (Various other groups of 'Peoples of the Sea' closely related to the Philistines settled further north along the coast.) Each of the five cities of the Philistines had its own 'lord' or ruler, and in each of the cities the Philistines lived according to their traditional customs, adapting themselves only where necessary to fit in with this new land in which they now lived. In military terms, they were very powerful. This was because they knew how to make iron tools and weapons. They had learnt this technique in Crete and brought the knowledge of it with them when they came to settle in Canaan. Iron weapons were much stronger and more effective than the bronze weapons which were all the Canaanites and Israelites knew how to make and use. The Philistines were well aware of the advantage their knowledge of how to work iron gave them. They refused to share the skill with the Israelites [see **1 Samuel 13:19–22**].

55

The misfortunes of Dan

Read Judges 18:1–2, 27–29
One of the first parts of the country where the coming of the Philistines affected the Israelites was in the land held by the tribe of Dan. The tribe of Dan had been settled in the coastal area of southern Canaan, 'with the ships', as the Song of Deborah puts it [**Judges 5:17**]. But this was precisely the region where the Philistines landed from the sea and established their five cities. In the stories of Samson [**Judges 13–16**], who was himself a member of the tribe of Dan, we see the Danites encountering the Philistines and gradually coming under pressure. Judges puts it: 'At this time the Philistines were ruling Israel.' [**Judges 14:4**]. In the stories of Samson and his immense strength we see what a valiant fight the Israelites put up. However, we also get the impression that the Philistines were much more powerful than the Israelites—Samson dies blinded and a prisoner, even though in his death he succeeds in killing many of the Philistines [**Judges 16:30**].

Eventually the tribe of Dan realised that their position was hopeless. The Philistines were too strong for them. The only solution left was to migrate from the lands they had settled near the sea and seek a new homeland. By this time most of the rest of Canaan was settled by the other Israelite tribes, who did not particularly want to share their territory with the Danites. So the tribe of Dan had to travel a considerable distance to find a new place to live—right up to the very north-west corner of Canaan. There there was a city called Laish, which was inhabited by some of the Canaanites. Far away from anywhere else, but in luxuriant and fertile countryside, the people of Laish really did not expect enemies to fall upon them. So the Danites were able to take Laish by surprise, burn it and kill its inhabitants. The writer of Judges makes it quite clear that he disapproves of the ferocity with which this was done. Afterwards the Danites settled in the city and renamed it Dan after themselves and their ancestor. It was considered the most northerly part of the land of Israel, and gradually the phrase 'from Dan to Beersheba' came into use to describe the land settled by the Israelites from north to south.

The fortunes of the Philistines

After the tribe of Dan had departed, the Philistines began to expand still further in the south of Canaan. It is clear that they captured Shiloh, the most important religious centre of the Israelites of that time. But once they had taken Shiloh, they had gained a foothold in the mountainous heartland of Canaan where the Israelites had previously been in firm control. Then the Philistines were able to move up northwards and seize the city of Beth-Shean near the Jordan River. This was a particularly significant move. For Beth-Shean stood at the point where the Jordan valley intersects with the valley of Jezreel which runs across Canaan from west to east. Control of Beth-Shean meant that the Philistines controlled the valley of Jezreel, and the very important routes that ran through it. It also meant that the Philistines had cut off the Israelite tribes in the north—Zebulun, Naphtali, Dan and Asher—from the tribes that lived south of the valley of Jezreel.

Philistine pottery.

Philistine writing?

We know all this from the Hebrew Scriptures themselves. However, the Philistines were even more successful than the Bible suggests. A few years ago, a mound called Tell Deir Alla, which is east of the River Jordan, was excavated. The archaeologists found there a number of tablets inscribed with a form of writing which has never been found before or since. For a variety of reasons it is thought to be 'Philistine writing', although this cannot be conclusively proved. But if it is Philistine writing, this would mean that the Philistines managed to settle and establish themselves even east of the River Jordan.

Hence they must have been in control of virtually the whole of the land of Canaan.

The Philistine legacy

As we shall see in the next section, the Philistine threat ultimately led to decisive changes in the way the Israelites organised themselves. Eventually the Israelites were able to counter-attack and defeat the Philistines. This happened in the time of David. But the Philistines were even then not forgotten. The name that the Romans gave to the land of Canaan a thousand years later was 'Palestine'. But 'Palestine' is just the way that the Romans said 'Philistine'. Sometimes even today the land of Canaan is called 'Palestine'. So right down to the present time the Philistines, that strange people different in so many ways from Israelites and Canaanites, are not forgotten in their new homeland far from the island of Crete!

A Phoenician warship. The Phoenicians and the Philistines were expert sailors, while the Israelites were not.

Some went down to the sea in ships?

All through their history the Israelites disliked and feared the sea. Unlike the Phoenicians and the Greeks, they never became sea-farers. When, in the time of Solomon, the Israelites and the Phoenicians had a joint trading venture down the Red Sea, it was the Phoenicians who provided the sailors. Why did the Israelites never really learn to go 'down to the sea in ships?' Part of the reason may lie in the devastating experience the Israelites had at the hands of the Philistines. Since these sinister people who gave the Israelites so much trouble had come upon them from the sea, the sea remained associated with danger and terror in the minds of the Israelites for many centuries to come. But there are other factors that we must also take into consideration. The coastline of Canaan is extremely straight and sandy. (This is because of the great quantity of sand washed down into the Mediterranean by the River Nile, which is then deposited on the coast of Canaan.) There are no good natural harbours along this straight coastline until you get north of Mount Carmel. So, with no natural harbours, there was not much incentive for the Israelites to learn the ways of the sea.

What is more, the Israelites shared with other peoples of the ancient Middle East the idea that the sea represented the chaotic powers that oppose the supreme god. We have seen how, in the stories from Ugarit, Yamm, the god of the sea, has to be conquered. The Hebrew word for sea is also *yamm*. The Israelites, too, felt that *yamm*, the sea, had to be conquered, though of course they regarded Yahweh, not Baal, as its conqueror.

Throughout the Hebrew Scriptures therefore the sea appears as a unknown and dangerous force. The writers of the psalms spoke of the fear the stormy sea inspired in men **[Psalm 107:23–32]**, and the story of the flood in Genesis is a powerful reminder of just how terrible the sea could be. Though the writers of the Bible were quite sure that God could control the sea, and the story of the crossing of the sea at the Exodus makes this clear, they still looked forward to a time when this fierce and turbulent force would no longer exist. And so in the vision of the new heaven and the new earth at the end of the Book of Revelation, St John promises: 'And there was no more sea' **[Revelation 21:1]**.

14 A king like the nations

No authority among the tribes

Life in the days of the judges was difficult for the Israelites. Not only was there the military threat that came from the Philistines, but the Israelite 'federation' was also threatened from within. The trouble was the lack of a really strong central authority which would be able to *compel* the tribes to act in accordance with Yahweh's laws if they were unwilling to do so. Gradually therefore a situation close to anarchy developed. We are given a particularly gruesome example [**Judges 19–20**]. A member of the tribe of Levi was travelling from Bethlehem to the hill country of Ephraim. Since the journey was too long to complete in one day, he stopped overnight in Gibeah, a city inhabited by people from the tribe of Benjamin. But here, instead of being treated hospitably by his fellow-Israelites, the Levite was seriously abused. His concubine, who was journeying with him, was seized by the men of the city and raped repeatedly until she died. In anger the Levite cut up her body into twelve pieces and sent a piece to each of the tribes. It was a dramatic act—the broken body of the concubine vividly symbolised the unity that all Israelites were supposed to share as the *one* people of Yahweh. But such unity obviously no longer existed if hospitality could be so seriously abused.

On this occasion the other Israelites *did* respond. Drastic punishment was meted out to the city of Gibeah where the outrage had occurred, and to the rest of the tribe of Benjamin who had been willing to let it happen. But the violence of the reprisal was even worse, for almost the whole of the tribe of Benjamin was exterminated. The Israelites began to realise that such a circle of violence and counter-violence could not be allowed to continue indefinitely, otherwise it would eventually destroy the whole of the Israelite people. And so after the story of the Levite's concubine and its after-

math, Judges closes with the warning words: 'There was no king in Israel at that time. Everyone did just as he pleased.' [**Judges 21:25**].

Samuel, the servant of the Lord

Read 1 Samuel 3:1–21

At this crucial stage in Israelite history, a leader who was a priest and a prophet, as well as a statesman and a judge, came on the scene. Samuel's life makes fascinating reading. He had been given to Yahweh's service even as a small child. His mother, Hannah, had been unable to have children. This was not only a sadness for her, but also a humiliation. For the other wife of Elkaneh, Hannah's husband, had produced several fine babies and lost no opportunity to mock Hannah about her childlessness. While the family was at pilgrimage at Shiloh, the city where the Ark of the Covenant was kept, for the annual Feast of Ingathering, Hannah prayed fervently for a child. She promised that if a child was born to her she would 'dedicate'

Traditionally, children have been very important in a Jewish family. This is why Hannah was mocked about her childlessness.

Stained-glass window in Lincoln Cathedral showing the child Samuel hearing God's call at the shrine while Eli is asleep.

the baby to the service of Yahweh in the shrine at Shiloh. Her prayer was heard, and a baby boy was born, whom she named Samuel. Hannah's song of rejoicing at the birth of Samuel [1 Samuel 2:1–10] reads almost like an earlier version of the Magnificat, the song of joy sung by Mary many centuries later [Luke 1:46–53].

When Samuel was a few years old, he was taken to Shiloh and left there in the care of Eli, the priest of the shrine. Samuel's duties were light: he tended the olive oil lamp which was placed next to the Ark of the Covenant. But as he grew older, he must have seen that all was not well at Shiloh. For although Eli, the old priest, was a good and holy man, Eli's sons, Hophni and Phineas, were evil and lawless. Eli was unable to control them. It was on a small scale the same kind of problem that the whole tribal 'federation' were experiencing. What is more, it seems as if the conduct of those who came to worship at the shrine was far from

satisfactory. All too often it turned to drunkenness and debauchery. In fact, when Samuel's mother had first come to pray for a child, she had been weeping so hard that Eli assumed she was drunk—so common was that kind of behaviour!

As always when things were at their worst, God himself took the initiative to make a new start. He called the young boy, Samuel, the most insignificant person at the shrine, to be his special servant and messenger. The call came while Samuel was watching over the Ark of the Covenant at night-time. At first he could not understand or believe Yahweh was speaking to him. But when he did comprehend, it was a sad message he had to hear. For at the same time that Samuel himself was appointed by Yahweh as a prophet, he also had to deliver the message that Yahweh wanted nothing more to do with the family of Eli [1 Samuel 3:10–14]. Their doom was sealed.

Prophet and seer

Samuel was one of the earliest of the Israelite prophets. In the centuries that followed, prophets and prophecy became very important in Israel. They deeply affected the history of the nation. Eventually the sayings, or oracles, of the most important of the prophets were collected, and prophetic 'books' began to appear. So, for example, we have the Book of Isaiah or the Book of Amos. (1 Samuel and 2 Samuel are not quite the Books of Samuel in exactly the same way as Isaiah is the Book of Isaiah—can you see the difference?) There are probably several reasons why prophecy began to appear in Israel at about the time of Samuel. The most important was that it met the critical need of that time.

What exactly was a prophet? There were many kinds, either working by themselves or as one of a group, living near a shrine or having no connection with any organised worship. But the essential thing about all Israelite prophets was that they believed they spoke the 'words of Yahweh'. The prophets were the 'mouth' that God used whenever he wanted to speak to his people. The people understood this in a very literal sense so, of course, this meant the prophets were extremely powerful people in Israelite society. You had to listen to what a prophet said, because you were really listening to God himself. And in turn this meant that whatever a prophet stated was bound to happen—because it was Yahweh himself speaking and he was in control of the events of history. So, for example, when Samuel tells Eli of the fate that will befall him and his family, Eli does not for a moment doubt Samuel's words, unpleasant though they may be **[1 Samuel 3:18]**.

All the same, it is probably a mistake to regard the prophets as *primarily* concerned with the future, certainly with the distant future. They were much more interested in the *present* historical situation in which they and their fellow Israelites found themselves. There were a variety of ways in which the prophets 'got in touch' with Yahweh. Sometimes they saw visions, sometimes they went into a kind of ecstatic trance, perhaps with the help of music, sometimes they just heard a voice. We read of Samuel using all three ways **[1 Samuel 3:21, 19:20, 8:7]**. In fact, on at least one occasion Samuel is called a 'seer' **[1 Samuel 9:11]**. Presumably this means that the people knew he 'saw' visions frequently.

Bands of prophets

Normally when we think of prophets we think of great individualists such as Samuel, Isaiah or Jeremiah. But it is clear from the Old Testament that bands or groups of prophets were also very common in ancient Israel. They make their first appearance in the story of Saul, who met a 'band of prophets' just after Samuel had anointed him. Later on Elijah and Elisha were often associated with bands of prophets.

Bands of prophets often had a connection with a sanctuary or place where the Israelites went to worship. Perhaps they helped provide the music for the worship, since they also used music to help them get into an ecstatic state and be able to prophesy [1 Samuel 10:5–13].

Such prophets were clearly regarded as rather strange people. When Saul himself starts to fall into a prophetic trance, the people around obviously disapprove of such a fine young man, of good family, being caught up with a bunch of hippies! 'Is Saul also among the prophets?', they ask themselves. It is not meant as a compliment.

One thing that may seem rather difficult to us: these prophets were paid for their prophesying. This could create problems. Sometimes it must have been a great temptation for them to prophesy what they knew their audience wanted them to hear! On the other hand, Samuel also received payment for his services as a 'seer' and a prophet, and no-one could ever accuse Samuel of sweetening his words to suit his audience's tastes.

Prophets sometimes went around in groups, speaking the 'words of Yahweh' while in an ecstatic trance.

The glory has departed!

Read 1 Samuel 4:1–22

For the next few years following his call by Yahweh, Samuel remained at Shiloh. Gradually, though, his reputation as a prophet began to spread among the Israelites. What Samuel said, happened! Perhaps it was just as well, for the Israelites were shortly to be in need of a reliable leader whom everyone could trust. The continual war with the Philistines had flared up again and, as before, the Israelites had come off decidedly the worse. They decided therefore to bring the Ark of the Covenant to the battlefield from its normal resting-place at Shiloh. It was not meant just as a morale booster. For the Israelites believed that in some mysterious way Yahweh was especially *there* in the Ark of the Covenant, and so by bringing the Ark to the battle they were bringing Yahweh himself to fight on their side. The Philistines seem to have thought so too, for when they saw that the Ark had arrived they cried, 'Woe is us . . . A god has come into the camp!'

However, what the Israelites had forgotten—as they were to forget so often in later history—was that Yahweh was not a god to be manipulated at people's whim. He was the 'I am who I am', the mysterious God who controlled and was not to *be* controlled. On this occasion the Israelites were resoundingly defeated, even though the Ark was with them. Worse than that, the Ark itself was captured by the Philistines. Hophni and Phineas, the worthless sons of Eli, who had brought the Ark up from Shiloh, were themselves killed and Eli their father

died of shock back at Shiloh when he heard the news. And the final act in the tragedy: Phineas' wife died giving birth prematurely to a baby boy. The baby was called Ichabod, a name which means 'the glory has departed', for everyone believed that through the capture of the Ark the glory or presence of Yahweh had completely left Israel.

Stolen goods bring bad luck

Read 1 Samuel 5:1–12

The Philistines found that possession of the Ark was a decidedly mixed blessing. In an account that seems like a bit of comic relief [**1 Samuel 5–6**] we read of the havoc it caused in the Philistine cities. Left overnight in the temple of Dagon (the Philistines' god) in Ashdod, Dagon's statue kept toppling over in front of it, as though Dagon himself wanted to bow down and worship this strange and powerful new god. And then a plague of boils and tumours broke out in Ashdod itself. The people of Ashdod then 'offered' the Ark to the Philistines at Gath, but it caused the same trouble there. Then it was shunted round most of the Philistine cities, an extremely unwelcome and troublesome gift.

The Philistines eventually decided there was nothing for it: the Ark would have to be returned to the Israelites—and they had better send along some offerings as well, to placate the god whom they had made so angry. So the Ark was sent back to the Israelites at Beth-Shemesh, along with golden images of the mice and the tumours that had plagued the Philistines.

Carving of the Ark at Capernaum. The Ark was very closely associated with Yahweh.

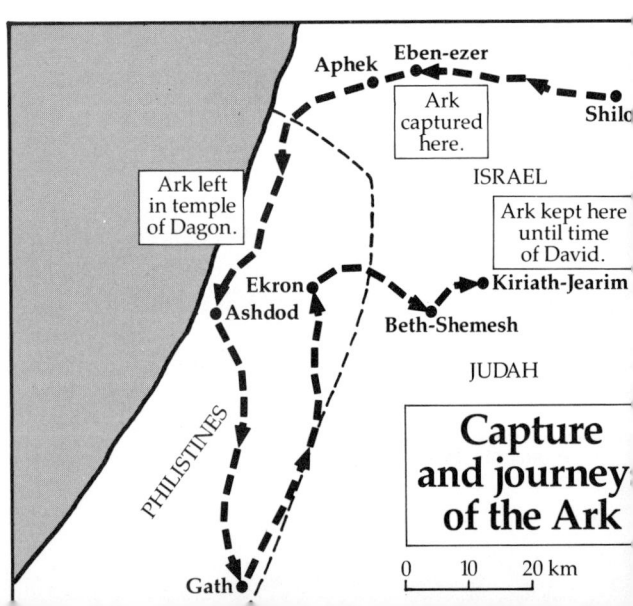

Capture and journey of the Ark

'We want a king!' But did Yahweh agree?

Even back among the Israelites the Ark could prove a dangerous thing to have around. For some of the Israelites at Beth-Shemesh made the mistake of looking into the Ark, and were struck down as a result—so they got rid of it fairly quickly too, handing it on to the Israelites of Kiriath-Jearim, a town in the mountains, where it was to remain for 20 years.

Underneath the humour—and the misadventures—of the story of the Ark's travels, there is a serious note. The Ark was dangerous, be-

cause it was so closely associated with the presence of a 'holy God' **[1 Samuel 6:20]**. We saw in section 6 what the people of the Hebrew Scriptures thought about holiness—it was like a two-edged sword, very powerful, but perilous if you came too close.

Give us a king!

In spite of the Ark's return to them, the Israelites knew that the old ways of doing things had to come to an end if the people were to survive. They needed a king—a strong man to whose authority all the Israelites would submit without question. The king would be able to organise the people to fight in a systematic and effective way. He would make sure that justice and law prevailed among all the Israelites—there would be no more taking the law into one's own hands, 'doing just as he pleased'. Other nations had kings and it seemed to work out well—why shouldn't the Israelites? So a delegation of Israelite leaders approached Samuel, who by now was acting as a 'judge' of the people as well as a prophet. 'Appoint for us a king to rule us like other countries have,' they said, 'Give us a king!' **[1 Samuel 8:5–6]**.

The word of God

What is a word? Is it something you mutter in a thoughtless moment and forget as soon as it has left your mouth? Not so in ancient Israel, where words had power. People believed that, once spoken, words could not easily be undone. Once they had left the speaker's mouth, they went on actually to bring about whatever he or she had spoken. In the story of Jacob and Esau **[Genesis 27:18–38]** Isaac gives Jacob by mistake the blessing that really belongs to the first-born. Even though he later realises what he has done, and even though it all happened because of Jacob's lies and deceit, it is still too late. The word of blessing cannot be undone. Jacob remains blessed, not Esau.

If all this is true of merely human words, how much more so of the words of Yahweh himself! When the prophets spoke the words which Yahweh put into their mouth, people believed that they were actually helping to

cause the events they prophesied. So it was very important that a prophet did not say anything unpleasant, and if he did, he could be accused, as the prophet Jeremiah was to be, of making the unpleasantness happen. On the other hand, whenever a prophet spoke of peace and prosperity, he helped that to happen as well. In a passage from the Hebrew Scriptures which comes from a long time after the life of Samuel, Yahweh himself describes his word in this way:

My word is like the snow and the rain
that come down from the sky to water the earth.
They make the crops grow
and provide seed for sowing and food to eat.
So also will be the word that I speak—
it will not fail to do what I plan for it;
it will do everything I sent it to do.

[Isaiah 55:10–11]

63

15   Saul, the tragic king

Two different accounts

Read 1 Samuel 8:4–22

What reply did Samuel give to the leaders of the Israelites when they came asking him to appoint a king? Here the story becomes rather complicated, for there appear to be two different versions of Samuel's response to the demand for a king. According to one account [**1 Samuel 8, 12**], Samuel is extremely angry with the people's request for a king. He regarded it as a vote of 'no confidence' in him and in the way he had 'judged' Israel. More than that, he felt it was disloyal to Yahweh. Like Gideon a hundred years or so before, Samuel believed that Yahweh was the *only* king the Israelites should have or want. To ask for a human king was like staging a *coup d'état* against God! However, according to the other account [**1 Samuel 9, 10**], Samuel is much more positive about the idea of a king. Indeed, according to this account, Samuel himself, under Yahweh's instructions, actually takes the initiative in the matter. God has taken pity on the people because he has seen how they have suffered at the hands of the Philistines. To stop this, therefore, he has commanded Samuel to anoint a young man, Saul, as king.

Why do we have these two very different accounts? In the first place, there were probably varying ideas being expressed at the time about whether or not it was a good idea to have a king. Many Israelites, perhaps the majority, were all in favour. Others, however, who were more conservative, felt that to have a king was somehow 'un-Israelite' and they liked the freedom that their tribal federation gave them. Moreover, they remembered how disastrous an experiment Abimelech's kingship at Shechem had been, and had no desire at all for a repeat performance. So the two different viewpoints expressed in the Hebrew Scriptures may well bear witness to these two different groups.

However, there is also another fact we have to take into account. The two different versions, for and against the kingship, may come from different periods in Israel's history. Perhaps the positive one comes from the very beginning of Saul's time as king, when great hopes were being placed in him. On the other hand, Saul's reign ended in failure. Perhaps the negative viewpoint comes from about that time, or perhaps even later.

Saul's lost asses

Read 1 Samuel 9–10:13

One day a young man went looking for some lost asses and found a kingdom! The 'positive' account of Saul's rise to power makes a vivid story for the reader to enjoy. While in search of his father's donkeys which disappeared, Saul asks the help of Samuel, the prophet or seer, whose job it is to know such things. Samuel reassures Saul that the donkeys are by now safely back at his father's house. But he has other, more important news for Saul and, before Saul leaves him the next morning, Samuel anoints him, pouring olive oil over his head as a sign that he is the one whom Yahweh has chosen to be the saviour of his people.

Samuel's choice of Saul is confirmed by several things that happen next. First, Saul falls in with a band of prophets shortly after leaving Samuel and begins to start prophesying himself [**1 Samuel 10:9–12**]. Later on, when the tribes meet at Mizpah, they decide to choose a king by lot and the choice falls upon Saul. Finally, Saul's claim to be king is confirmed by a resounding victory over the Ammonites, and after this no-one wants to dispute his right to be their ruler [1 Samuel 11:11–15].

Samuel rejects Saul

Read 1 Samuel 15:1–23
To begin with, all goes extremely well for Saul and his reign. He defeats the Philistines and drives them out of the central highlands. Incidentally, this is the last time in the Bible that the Israelites are called Hebrews. The Philistines refer to them as Hebrews [1 Samuel 14:11] and the word has the same derogatory sense about it as it did when it was used by the Egyptians at the time of the Exodus.

Saul's victory over the Philistines is resounding, and it is followed by further defeats of the Ammonites, Moabites and Edomites. But then the bright optimism with which Saul's reign had begun starts to fade. For Saul fell out with Samuel. Once again there are two accounts giving somewhat different reasons for the quarrel. In one account, Saul offered a sacrifice without waiting for Samuel—thus taking over a job that really belonged only to Samuel and those who were priests like him [1 Samuel 13:8–15]. According to the other account, Saul disobeyed Samuel's instructions in a battle with the Amalekites, a long-standing enemy of the Israelites (see section 10). He did not keep up the traditions of the 'holy war' in which everything was totally destroyed. Instead he spared Agag, king of the Amalekites, and kept the best of the sheep and oxen as well [1 Samuel 15:1–35].

Both stories, though, are really making the same point: the quarrel between Samuel and Saul was really over the question of *authority*. Did Saul, now that he had become king, have the right to change the laws and traditions of the Israelites? Most Canaanite kings felt that they themselves were above the law—they *made* the law. Perhaps Saul felt that now this was his right as well. But Samuel felt differently. As far as he was concerned, the final source of authority was still Yahweh and the laws and customs that Yahweh had decreed in the wilderness. Saul had to obey them as much as any other Israelite. And if Saul thought otherwise, he was too dangerous to have around. He had better go.

Samuel anointing Saul.

The anointed of God

Saul, and later David and most of the other kings of Israel, were anointed before they began to reign. In the rite of anointing, pure oil was poured over their heads. But not only kings were anointed. We also read in the Hebrew Scriptures of prophets and priests being anointed at times. Probably the custom of anointing the leaders of the Israelites was meant to signify that these people belonged in a special way to Yahweh. They were his 'vassals' and were being commissioned for his service. They were also under his particular protection.

Often we read that when a person is anointed, at the same time the 'Spirit of Yahweh' comes upon him. The spirit of Yahweh is a way of describing the visible power of Yahweh—it is like a strong wind that bowls people over. When the spirit of Yahweh has taken possession of someone, it means that that person is so completely Yahweh's vassal that he or she has been 'taken over' by him; Yahweh is 'in' that person so that he or she can do Yahweh's will.

The Hebrew word for 'anointed one' is 'Messiah'. So when much later the Israelites were hoping for a Messiah, they were actually looking for someone who would be anointed by Yahweh to act as his servant and carry out his instructions. The Messiah, too, would be filled with the spirit of Yahweh [Isaiah 11:2]. (See *Jesus and the Gospels*, pp. 53–54.)

Saul and David

Read 1 Samuel 18:6–16

Saul's quarrel with Samuel was a turning point in his career. From then on until his death it was a period of steady decline. Part of Saul's problem was undoubtedly David, for after Samuel rejected Saul he chose David, a young shepherd from Bethlehem. He announced that Yahweh had anointed David in Saul's stead. The stories of the relations between Saul and David are as ambiguous as the tales of Samuel and Saul. Perhaps this is because some of the stories were written down by friends of Saul, and others by friends of David. It seems that David joined Saul's army. He became famous as a result of his single-handed combat with the Philistine giant Goliath. He also became extremely friendly with Jonathan, Saul's son. But soon Saul became afraid: David was no longer an asset, a captain who contributed to Saul's own success. Instead he had become a threat and a rival for the people's affection. It must have been hard for Saul to listen to the chant that went up, 'Saul has slain his thousands, and David his ten thousands.' [**1 Samuel 18:7**].

Suddenly Saul had had enough. He tried to kill David, who fled for safety, ironically enough to the shelter of the Philistines. But

Stained glass by Burne-Jones depicting David's victory over Goliath. David's successes and charisma threatened Saul.

David as an open enemy was even more dangerous to Saul than he had been as a rival in his own camp. Now he gathered a band of men of his own and harassed Saul in guerrilla attacks from behind the Philistine lines. In fact, on several occasions he had Saul within his grasp and could have killed him. But it wasn't only a physical threat that David presented. For Saul had once upon a time loved David, and the bitter quarrel prayed upon his mind. Eventually he became mentally and emotionally ill, and totally unfit to lead his armies and the Israelites.

The last few years of Saul's life, related in the closing chapters of **1 Samuel**, were a sorry story. Gradually Saul's conquests slipped from his grasp. The Philistines returned to the fight, stronger and more threatening than ever. Saul decided upon a last stand to try and shift the Philistines from their strongholds in the valley of Jezreel through which they had a stranglehold upon the Israelites. But even as he went into his final battle, Saul knew that he was doomed. The night before he had gone to consult a witch [**1 Samuel 28:8–19**]—itself an indication of how low he had sunk, for witchcraft was expressly forbidden by Yahweh. The ghost of the now dead Samuel rose from the earth.

The valley of Jezreel seen from Mount Tabor. It was here that Saul met his doom.

Even dead, he had no good news for Saul—death alone awaited him. The next morning it happened exactly as Samuel had predicted. In the battle with the Philistines, Saul was badly wounded and committed suicide rather than be taken prisoner. Saul's son Jonathan was also killed and the Israelite army was scattered. And at the end of the life of the man who had been chosen to save his people from the Philistines, the Philistines were in complete control.

The tragic drama

Have you ever read Shakespeare's *Hamlet* or *Macbeth*? Or perhaps the Greek drama *Oedipus the King*? In all of these dramatic tragedies there is a figure whose greatness is the cause of his downfall. The very qualities that contribute to his success also lead finally to his collapse and failure. And frequently the beginning of the end came as the result of a moment of hubris or pride, when the hero of the story has become so confident that he believes the rules of ordinary mortals don't apply to him any longer. When you read the Hebrew Scriptures, Saul and his story feel rather like a tragic drama. In his time of greatness Saul overstretched himself—and that eventually led to his bitter and tragic end.

There were also other reasons for Saul's ultimate lack of success. He was Israel's first king (other than Abimelech) and the Israelites took time to get used to the idea of having a

Stained glass in Chartres Cathedral showing Saul taking his own life.

king at all. And perhaps many people weren't really sure just *what* Saul was. Was he a king? Or was he the last of the judges? Or was he a prince—somewhere in between a king and a judge? In fact, the stories about Saul often prefer to refer to him as a prince rather than a king. And then there is the question of whether *all* the Israelite tribes accepted his authority all the time. For if one reads the stories about Saul rather closely, one gets the feeling that it was really only the tribe of Benjamin, Saul's own tribe, who were wholly behind him. So Saul indeed had many problems to contend with!

In true tragic style, the death of Saul is mourned in verse and song. In life there may have been enmity between Saul and David, but David's lament over Saul and Jonathan after their death is one of the most beautiful pieces of poetry in the Hebrew Scriptures.

> On the hills of Israel our leaders are dead
> The bravest of our soldiers have fallen
> Do not announce it in Gath
> or in the streets of Ashkelon.
> Do not make the women of Philistia glad;
> do not let the daughters of pagans rejoice.
>
> May no rain or dew fall on Gilboa's hills;
> may its fields be always barren!
> For the shields of the brave lie there in disgrace;
> the shield of Saul is no longer polished with oil. (. . .)
>
> Saul and Jonathan, so wonderful and dear;
> together in life, together in death;
> swifter than eagles, stronger than lions.
>
> Women of Israel, mourn for Saul!
> He clothed you in rich scarlet dresses
> and adorned you with jewels and gold.
>
> The brave soldiers have fallen,
> their weapons abandoned and useless.

[2 Samuel 1:19–21, 23–24, 27].

16   David and his city

David's moment did not come the very instant that Saul died. Wisely, he knew that it was better to bide his time. Eventually the Israelites would need to come and seek his help. So, although he was anointed as king at Hebron, in the south of the country, after Saul's death, he only ruled as king over the people of Judah, his own tribe. The rest of Israel chose one of Saul's remaining sons, Ishbosheth, as their ruler. But gradually David's charisma and obvious success led to people switching sides. After seven years there was a rebellion against Ishbosheth, and the Israelites came to David in Hebron and asked him to rule over them all. David's moment had now arrived.

The capture of Jerusalem

Read 2 Samuel 5:6–10
David was a skilful politician and did not intend to repeat the mistakes that Saul had made. He knew that it was vital to secure the loyalty of all the tribes. Even though he was naturally particularly sympathetic to people from Judah, his own tribe, he understood that it was essential to be as impartial as possible. One pressing question was where he should locate his capital. Hebron, where he had lived for the last seven years, was unsatisfactory. Not only was it identified in people's minds especially with Judah, but it was also geographically inconvenient now that David was king over *all* Israel. In one bold move he solved the problem—and in the process gave to his people a city which has come to symbolise people's hope for peace and unity. David captured Jerusalem.

Jerusalem with a city that had so far eluded the Israelites. It was well fortified and easily defensible and so had remained in the control of its original inhabitants, the Jebusites, a group of the Canaanites, ever since the Israelites had come into the land. The capture of Jerusalem was a difficult task, but the prize was worth the risk.

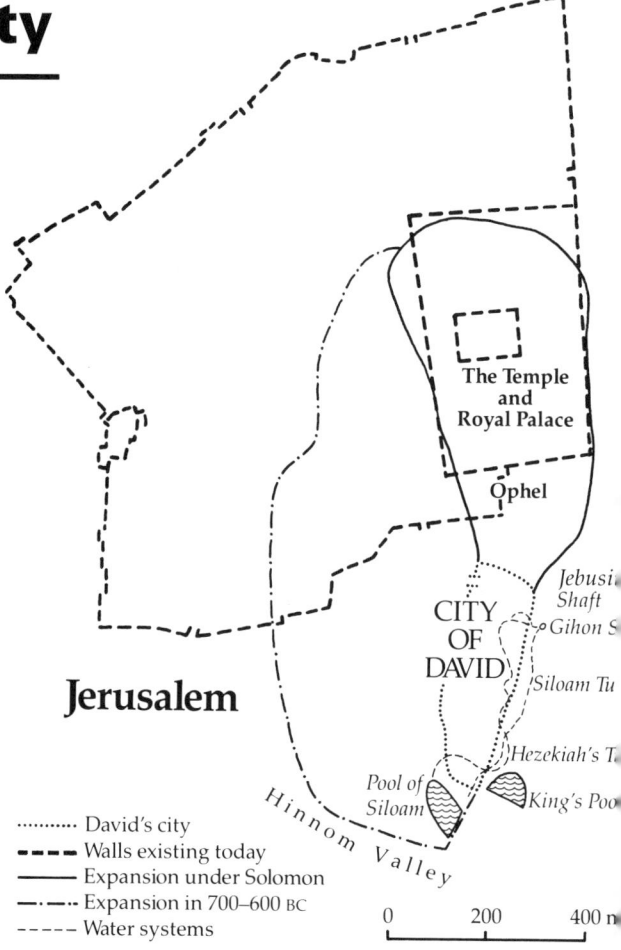

Jerusalem

- ·········· David's city
- ▬ ▬ ▬ Walls existing today
- ▬▬▬ Expansion under Solomon
- ▬·▬·▬ Expansion in 700–600 BC
- ▬ ▬ ▬ Water systems

0   200   400 m

Up the water shaft

Look at the map of Jerusalem on this page. It is important to realise that Jerusalem at the time of David was not exactly where the walled city of Jerusalem stands today. It was on a hill which extends just south of the present-day walls of Jerusalem. On the map the limits of David's Jerusalem are marked by a dotted line. The hill on which Jerusalem was built was extremely steep, so steep in fact that it was not ideal for the site of a city. Why then had the Jebusites built their city on *this* hill and not on one of a number of other hills in the area where building might have been easier? The answer lies at the foot of the hill, for there, tucked away in the side of the rock, was a spring, the Gihon spring, the only source of fresh water in the area.

We have already seen in section 11 how important water was to the people of Canaan. The long dry months of the summer mean that water becomes very precious during this time. Although it might be possible for farmers and villagers to collect enough rain-water during the winter months to help see them through the summer, for city-dwellers this was not the case. A city could only grow up where there was a spring, a source that would give the people fresh water all year round. So Jerusalem had been built near the Gihon.

The citizens of Jerusalem also had to ensure that they could always get at their water-supply. For the spring was at the foot of the hill, outside the walls which had been built to defend the city in time of siege. To ensure constant access—even in times of war—the Jebusites of Jerusalem had designed an ingenious solution. They sunk a vertical shaft down from inside the walls to the same level as the spring. Then, working from the spring itself, they bored a tunnel into the hillside until it met the shaft. Now, the water from the spring ran along the tunnel until it came to the bottom of the shaft, while from the top of the shaft the inhabitants of the city could lower buckets to collect their water in times of war as well as peace. Of course, no-one would be able to climb the water-shaft and get into the city that way, for it was far too steep. At least the Jebusites thought so, and left the shaft unguarded! That was their downfall, for that was precisely the way David and his men managed to get into the city and seize it when and where its defenders were least expecting it.

Israelite waterworks

The Jebusite water shaft was clearly not completely successful, since David and his men had actually used it to get into the city. After David's time it does not appear to have been used a great deal again. In the days of David and Solomon, since the country was at peace, the inhabitants of Jerusalem could always walk outside the city gates and collect their water.

Three hundred years later it was a different story. Then, in the time of King Hezekiah (about 710 BC), the Assyrians were threatening to besiege the city, and the water problem once more became pressing. Hezekiah's response was an engineering feat which was admired in the ancient world and even recorded in the Bible [2 Kings 20:20]. He dug a tunnel that ran right under the hill on which Jerusalem was built and came out the other side, in an area which lay within the city walls. As a result the waters of the Gihon spring were diverted through the tunnel out into a man-made pool, called the Pool of Siloam. Here the inhabitants of Jerusalem could safely collect it. For security's sake, the original opening of the Gihon spring was completely covered over, so no-one would know where the tunnel began. Hezekiah's great achievement was commemorated on a stone discovered last century in the tunnel itself.

Hezekiah's tunnel ended at the Pool of Siloam, which can still be seen today.

Jerusalem however, was not the only city in Canaan where elaborate water-works were designed and built. We know of water tunnels and shafts in Gibeon, Gezer, Megiddo and Hazor. The great water tunnel of Megiddo is especially impressive. It may date from the time of Solomon, David's son.

City of David

After Jerusalem's capture, David did not kill the inhabitants. That policy, somewhat unusual in the warfare of those days, was quite deliberate. David was trying to create a new kingdom in which both Canaanites and Israelites could share. In that kingdom Jerusalem had a definite role to play. It was to become David's capital, the City of David because, having been previously Canaanite, it was in a sense 'neutral' territory. It had not been previously associated with any *one* of the twelve Israelite tribes, so there would be no question of tribal jealousy when it was chosen as the capital. It was to be the Canberra or Ottawa of David's Israel, a neutral capital that helped to unite different and sometimes hostile groups.

Dancing before the Ark

Read 2 Samuel 6:16–23
After he had taken Jerusalem, to set the seal on its new importance, David had the Ark of the Covenant brought up from Kiriath-Jearim to a resting place in the capital. It came in a great procession, with the music of cymbals and lutes, and singing and dancing. David himself danced in the procession—much to the disgust of Michal, his wife, who felt that it was undignified for a king to clown around in this way. All the same, it was a great moment in David's

King David dancing in front of the Ark of the Covenant.

life when he brought the Ark up to Jerusalem, for he believed that now the presence and blessing of Yahweh himself was associated both with this city, and with himself as its king.

David thought of building a temple, a 'house' for the Ark. That was an ambition of his that he did not fulfil—his son Solomon was to do so instead. However, towards the end of his life David did buy a site just outside the city where sacrifice could be offered to Yahweh, and he set up an altar there.

Absalom, my son!

David was extremely successful. He defeated the Philistines once and for all and drove them right down to the coastal plain from where they were never really able to trouble the Israelites again. The rest of the Canaanite cities in the land, which had so far held out against the Israelites, now also became part of his kingdom. But his military campaigns also stretched far beyond the borders of Canaan, past Dan and Beersheba. Soon all the neighbouring kings, of Ammon, Moab, Edom and Damascus, became David's vassals, bringing him tribute each year. David had created an empire to bequeath to the son who was to succeed him.

But which son? David's personal life was far from happy. He had many sons by several different wives and there was a good deal of envy and rivalry among them. Which of them would

'Jerusalem of gold', with a view over the Dome of the Rock and Temple area.

succeed their father after his death? As David grew older, the tensions became more acute. Eventually Absalom, one of David's sons, broke into open rebellion. For a while it looked as though victory would go his way—David had to flee from the capital. But a small band remained loyal to David, and soon the tide was turned. Now it was Absalom's turn to try and escape, but he was not so fortunate. With David's men hot in pursuit, he got caught up by an oak tree! It was an easy matter for Joab, David's captain, to put an arrow into his heart.

Absalom had been a traitor, but David had not wanted his son to die. 'O my son! My son Absalom! Absalom, my son! If only I had died in your place, my son! Absalom, my son!' [**2 Samuel 18:33**].

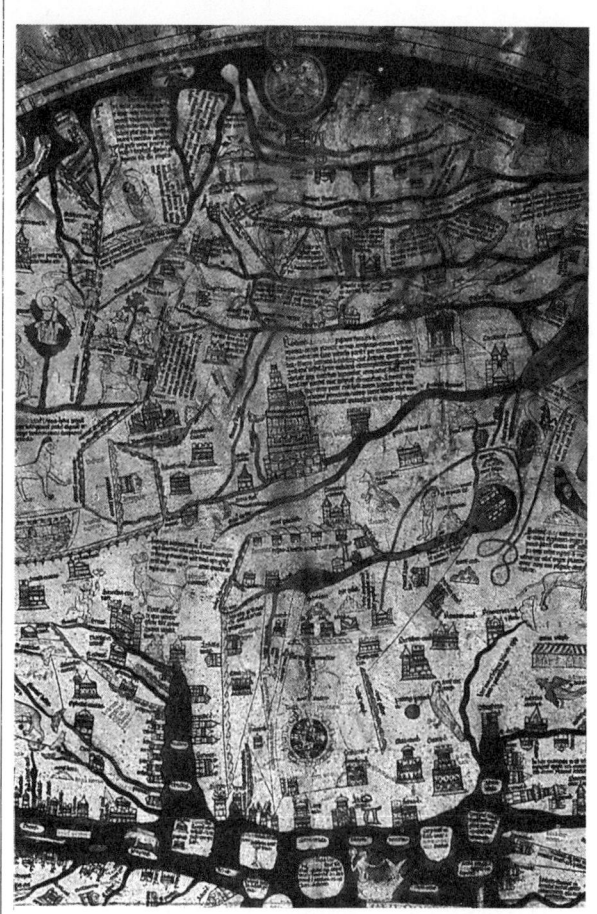

This medieval map from Hereford Cathedral puts Jerusalem at the centre of the world. That was a sign of how important Jerusalem was felt to be—and still is.

Jerusalem, City of Gold

There is a Jewish proverb about Jerusalem: 'Ten measures of beauty gave God to the world; nine to Jerusalem and one to all the rest. Ten measures of sorrow gave God to the world; one to the world beyond her walls, but nine to Jerusalem.' A slight exaggeration, perhaps, but not much. Jerusalem is a very beautiful city. The stones glow golden in the afternoon sun. It is also a city that has great significance for many people—for Jews, Christians and Muslims. But, for these very reasons, it has been fought over a great number of times. Its beauty has led to its sorrow. It is particularly sad, because the name 'Jerusalem' seems to mean 'city of peace', but Jerusalem has hardly ever lived up to its name.

Nevertheless, the city of Jerusalem remains a powerful symbol for religious people. Running through the Bible there is expressed the hope that one day Jerusalem will indeed be a place of peace to which all peoples will be able to go and worship God.

'Arise Jerusalem, and shine like the sun;
The glory of the Lord is shining on you!
(. . .)
Nations will be drawn to your light,
And kings to the dawning of your new day.

[**Isaiah 60:1, 3**].

71

17 David and his heirs

Israel becomes a nation

In the 250 years or so between the time the Israelites came into the land of Canaan and the end of the reign of David, Israelite society underwent many drastic changes. So did the understanding of what 'Israel' itself meant. A basic change had been the shift in lifestyle: nomadic shepherd to settled agriculturalist. But gradually other changes occurred as well. When the Israelites had come to Canaan, they had been organised in tribes—with every member of the tribe having an equal say in how the tribal affairs were to be run. There had been officially a 'federation' of the twelve tribes but, as we have seen, this was really fairly loose in form. The main focus of unity of the tribes was their common faith in Yahweh.

By the end of the lifetime of David all this had changed. Now there was an obvious and visible focus of unity for the Israelites—the person of the king, to whom members of all the tribes were (at least in theory!) completely loyal. And we can no longer say that all people were entirely equal either before the law or before Yahweh, for David and his heirs had a special role to play both in the laws and in the

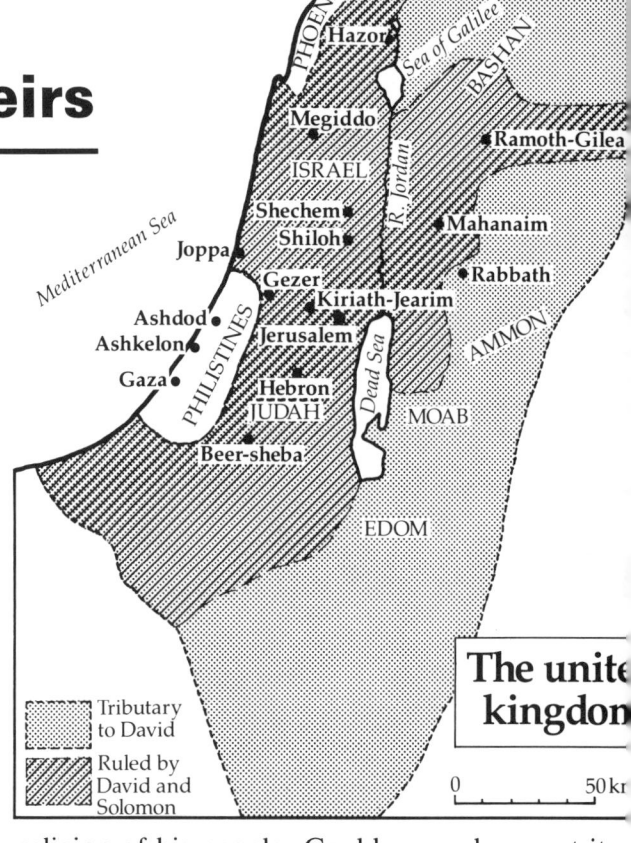

The united kingdom

Tributary to David

Ruled by David and Solomon

0   50km

religion of his people. Could we perhaps put it another way—'monarchy' had replaced 'federal republic'?

And the word 'Israel' itself—what changes it had undergone! Originally Israel had been a name given to one man, Jacob, after the momentous night on which he fought with God. Then it had been extended to include Israel's sons and his wider family, and so had become the name of a tribal group. At Sinai it had changed again, and the word Israel now referred to a people—the people who worshipped Yahweh—though, of course, most of them were also descendants of the original Israel. After the people had come into the land of Canaan, the word Israel was used to describe the twelve tribes acting together. But at the time of David, the word underwent a further change, for now it meant a people living in a land which for the first time they controlled completely—in other words, a 'nation' in the fullest possible sense.

Previously we have talked about the Israelites living in the land of Canaan. Now, however, we can say that they lived in the land of Israel. Israel is the name of a country and a state as well as of a people.

Conservatives versus radicals

It is quite certain that all these major changes did not take place in Israelite society without a great deal of opposition. We have already seen, when we were looking at the story of Saul, that there was a strong 'conservative' party. In the time of David this conservative party was still there, but much less influential. That was partly because Saul had 'paved the way' for David, and also because David was a much stronger character than Saul. All the same, there are little hints that surface from time to time. Michal's disapproval of David's dance before the Ark—was it perhaps that she disapproved of these new-fangled goings-on? Nathan's refusal to allow David to build a temple—there was no need, as he saw it, because Yahweh had managed quite well without one up to now. That perpetual bickering among David's sons—they became quite expert at playing off the conservative opposition to David for their own benefit. And towards the end of David's life his attempt to carry out a census of the people for purposes of taxation met with violent opposition. It was seen by many as just another way of the king tightening his grip and interfering with the traditional way of life of the Israelite people [2 Samuel 24:1–9].

The king: son of God

When David captured Jerusalem and made it his capital, he found that the people who were living there had very definite ideas about the role and position of a king.

Once again, as in section 11, the Ugaritic texts can come to our help. This time we can use them to find out what exactly the Canaanites of the land would have thought about kings. In Canaanite society, kings were felt to be very special people. Though they were regarded as human beings (unlike the Pharaohs of Egypt, who were felt to be actually divine—see section 4), kings were felt to be different in important ways from other human beings. They had a special relationship with the gods. This was so close that sometimes Canaanite kings are called 'son of god'. But, more than this, the kings of Canaan were felt to be the channel through which the ordinary people of the land 'com-

Charlemagne, a great king of France. At that time most European monarchs felt they had a 'divine right' to do as they liked.

municated' with the gods and received whatever gifts and blessings the gods had for them.

There is a technical term for this way of thinking about kings. It is called 'sacral kingship'. For people who believe in sacral kingship the king becomes an intermediary between the divine and human worlds. For it is *through* the person of the king that the gods give peace, prosperity and justice to the people ruled by that king. It also means that the king becomes an indispensable person: for if the king is absent or unwell, the people themselves will also suffer. In the stories from Ugarit we can read of a King Keret who falls sick. But King Keret's sickness has devastating consequences for the people of Ugarit. The earth itself 'sickens' and the plants wither and die. The skies become empty of birds, and the animals no longer bear young. Even the citizens of Ugarit begin to fall ill themselves. King Keret must get better!

Sacral kingship may seem to us today to be a very strange and unlikely way of looking at the world, but it was very popular throughout the ancient world. In parts of our world today there is still this concept of a king as a sacral person. Among the Shilluk people of Sudan, the Reth or king of the people must be healthy—or otherwise his people and his land will fall ill. The Reth has to show how fit he is by being the first person up in the morning and the last person to bed at night!

David coveted Bathsheba, who was Uriah's wife. He arranged for Uriah to die so that he could marry her. However, not even kings were above Yahweh's law.

The covenant with David

Read 2 Samuel 7:1–17

Though it may have appeared unnecessary to many of the Israelites for David and his family to begin to think about themselves in this way, a belief in sacral kingship does have some important practical advantages. For it so emphasises the importance of the person of the king that the king really does become a focus of unity for his people. No-one will dare to start a rebellion, because they are afraid of bringing down the anger of the gods on their heads. At least that is the theory!

So in the time of David, the Israelites began to take over some of the Canaanite ways of thinking about kingship. Of course they never believed that the king was divine—only Yahweh could be that. But they did think of the king as Yahweh's special representative, almost his 'vice-regent' on earth. And they believed that the king was Yahweh's son—not physically, but having a special place in his affections. Because they were Israelites and therefore used to thinking about their relationship with God in terms of 'covenants', they began to realise that Yahweh had made a special 'covenant' with David. We can read of the making of the Davidic covenant in **2 Samuel 7**. David has just held a discussion with the prophet Nathan about building a 'house' for

Yahweh. Nathan's reply is that Yahweh doesn't need a house, but he will build David a 'house' instead. In other words, Yahweh promised to make David's kingdom strong and stable and to ensure that one of David's sons would become king after him. Once again, as in the case of Abraham, we have here Yahweh making a covenant with one individual person—even though this is a very important person. The covenant with David does not mean that the covenant at Sinai was no longer valid—both 'covenants' were to remain important in the coming year, at least in and around Jerusalem. All the same, it does seem that people may have preferred to concentrate on one or the other of the covenants, either the 'Davidic covenant' or the 'Sinai covenant'. This must have led to tension at times.

The wife of Uriah

Although Yahweh had made a special covenant with David, this did not mean that David could behave just as he liked. In case we should think so, the Hebrew Scriptures tell us of an incident in the life of David to make it quite clear this was not the case. A beautiful woman, Bathsheba, had caught David's eye. Unfortunately for David she was already married—to Uriah, a captain in David's army. But David was determined to have Bathsheba for himself, and eventually organised Uriah's death. He had him deliberately placed in the front line of the fighting troops in the war against the Ammonites. As expected, Uriah was killed, and after a discreet interval David was able to marry Bathsheba. He thought he had got away with it. Nobody had guessed—or if they had, they would surely not dare accuse the king.

You are the man

Read 2 Samuel 12:1–15

Here David miscalculated. His deed had not escaped Yahweh. No sooner had David married Bathsheba than Nathan the prophet appeared. He did not accuse David directly—for otherwise he would never have got a hearing. Instead he told a parable: There were two men, one rich, the other poor. Although the rich man had many sheep, he envied the poor man his one little ewe lamb. One day he stole it. David's anger was aroused by the wickedness of the theft, 'Let the thief die,' he said. Nathan's reply was swift. 'You are the man.' **[2 Samuel 12:7]**. Precisely because David was the king and had received Yahweh's special blessing, his theft of Bathsheba could not go unpunished—their first child would die.

In many countries of the ancient Middle East, Nathan's bold attack on David would not have succeeded. Kings felt able to make or break laws at will. But in Israel things were different.

The Ten Commandments applied to the king as much as to anyone else—indeed, the king had a special responsibility to ensure they were strictly kept. And it is not an accident that, once there were kings in Israel, we hear much more about prophets like Samuel, Nathan, and later Elijah. For the absolute power in Israel that the kings now had meant that there was an important job for prophets—to be the only people who dared to bring a message straight from Yahweh and say to the kings as often as necessary: 'You are the man!'

The son of David

After David's death, the Israelites looked back on his reign with a great deal of nostalgia. Nobody pretended that David had been perfect, but even his failings made him seem more human. You could almost love David *because* of his faults! Solomon, David's son, for all his grandeur and magnificence, couldn't quite manage to live up to his father's image. He just didn't have the common touch that David had. And after Solomon, the glory soon vanished and Israel, instead of having a great empire, quickly became a tiny kingdom struggling for survival (see *The Progress of God's People* in this series). Gradually, therefore, people's hopes turned towards the future. One day,

they believed, there would be another king in Israel who would bring back prosperity to the land. He would have an empire at least as great as that David had won. Like David, he would be 'anointed' by Yahweh, and so the name given to this king to come was the 'Messiah', which meant the 'anointed one'. And, since it was believed that the Messiah would be one of David's descendants, he could also be referred to as the 'son of David'.

The Israelites also remembered that David had had a specially close relationship with Yahweh. The Messiah would be just the same. So, like David, the Messiah would be the 'son of God' and be the one who linked God and people.

18 Solomon and his glory

Solomon was born to all the advantages for which David had had to fight. He was David's son by Bathsheba—the second son, for the first child had died soon after birth. He had many good qualities: he was skilful, intelligent, well able to move in a world of trade and international diplomacy. Yet for all his so-called 'wisdom', he wasn't really wise! He had inherited a great empire that had been built by David, so he did not need to wage wars. He could concentrate on developing the country and building up its trade. But he went about this in an autocratic way; he did not show the tact his father David had done. He was unjust and unfair. The end result was that as soon as Solomon died the empire fell apart, and the 'golden age' came to a sudden end.

The land of the Queen of Sheba

Read 1 Kings 10
All too frequently in its history the geographical location of the land of Canaan has been to its disadvantage. It is a kind of 'land bridge' situated on the routes that run between Africa, Asia and Arabia, between Egypt and Mesopotamia. Across this land bridge armies have marched to war a great number of times, leaving a trail of destruction behind them. The reign of Solomon was the one time in the history of Israel when the geographical situation of the land proved of immense advantage.

Remember that the kings of Damascus, Ammon, Moab and Edom were vassals of David and after him therefore of Solomon. If you look at the map on this page, you will see that this meant that Solomon completely controlled all the trade routes that ran between the north and the south of the ancient Middle East. If you wanted to transport frankincense from Arabia to Mesopotamia, or bring horses from the land of the Hittites down to Egypt, you had to do so

using roads that were controlled by Solomon. You also had to pay his customs tolls. And because Solomon's empire sat so firmly astride the trade routes, it also meant that goods from all over the ancient world found their way to Jerusalem itself. **1 Kings 10**—part of the state records of Solomon—gives us a long list of all these delicacies that Solomon's trading ventures had brought to his court.

However, goods were not only brought by land, for Solomon also went into partnership with Hiram, King of Tyre, and sent ships far

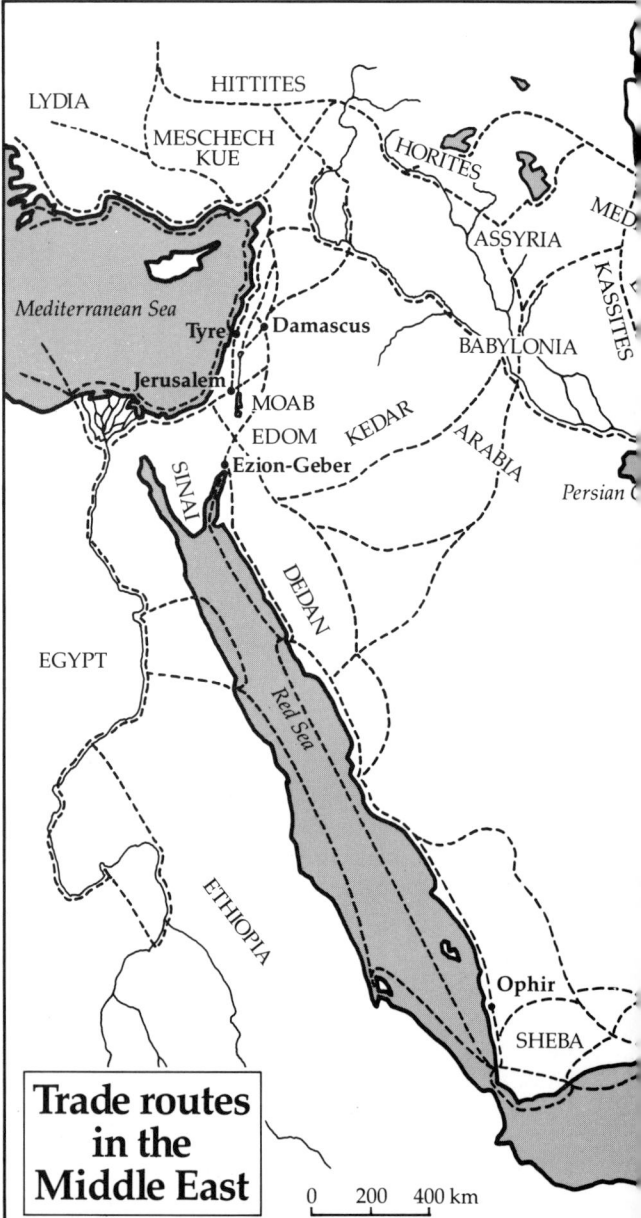

Trade routes in the Middle East

0   200   400 km

across the seas. Hiram and the people of Tyre provided the expertise, for the Israelites had never been good sailors. Solomon provided the ships and the port Ezion-Geber, at the northern tip of the Red Sea, which his father David had taken from the Edomites. From Ezion Geber Solomon's and Hiram's men sailed far south, bringing back valuable spices, incense, gold, precious stones and 'almug' wood. The ships certainly sailed as far as Ophir in the far south-west corner of Arabia (present-day Yemen). Possibly they journeyed on to the Somali coast on the eastern shores of Africa, and it is even conceivable that they used the monsoon winds to reach India and bring back spices, especially the prized cinnamon.

Trade missions came to Jerusalem to discuss tariffs and future ventures. One such mission has been recorded in the Hebrew Scriptures, for it was surely to discuss their mutual trade that the Queen of Sheba travelled 2400 km from South Arabia and marvelled at the splendour she saw at Solomon's court.

The gift of wisdom

Read 1 Kings 4:29–34
Other more intangible benefits flowed to Solomon's court. Solomon had extremely good relations with the Egyptians—for the first and only time in history an Israelite king was treated as an equal by the Pharaohs. He married a daughter of Pharaoh, who brought with her as her dowry the city of Gezer in southern Canaan. Back in section 4 we looked at the study of 'wisdom' practised by the Egyptians. We saw that it was the art of getting on in life and ensuring that the government was running smoothly. Solomon began to run his court along Egyptian lines. We are told the names of some members of Solomon's bureaucracy **[1 Kings 4:1–6]**. Probably Solomon brought to Jerusalem Egyptian advisors to teach himself and his people 'wisdom'. Remember how the 'wisdom training' of the scribes in Egypt involved the study of natural history, botany and zoology. Solomon himself, it seems, excelled in this kind of wisdom. 'He composed 3000 proverbs and more than a thousand songs. He spoke of trees and plants, from the Lebanon cedars to the hyssop that grows on walls; he talked about

Two women fight over a baby. Which was the real mother? Read 1 Kings 3:16–28 and see how Solomon was 'wise' enough to decide between them.

animals, birds, reptiles and fish. Kings all over the world heard of his wisdom and sent people to listen to him.' **[1 Kings 4:32–34]**.

Solomon's interest in wisdom has led to much of the 'wisdom literature' in the Hebrew Scriptures being associated with his name. The Book of Proverbs is attributed to Solomon and so also is a book called Ecclesiastes. (Not everything in these two books was actually written by Solomon, though some of the Proverbs certainly were.)

Solomon's court was a literate place—people now knew and made use of the art of writing. Incidentally, it was far easier to learn to read and write in Hebrew, the language of the Israelites, than it was in the language of the Egyptians and the people of Mesopotamia. In Hebrew there are only 22 symbols to learn. The reason we know so much about the reign of Solomon is because, for the first time in Israelite history, people began to keep detailed written records. Probably it was also Solomon who ensured that the story of David's reign was written down. He had a personal motive for this, for he wanted to explain how it was that he, rather than one of David's other sons, had come to the throne.

Solomon's chariot cities

Read 1 Kings 9:15–19
As well as all his international contacts and ventures, Solomon also maintained an extensive building and development programme within Israel itself. He built himself a splendid palace of cedar wood in Jerusalem and enlarged the walls of the city. He also built a temple for Yahweh (see section 19). Outside Jerusalem he began to mine copper in the southern Negev desert near Ezion-Geber and the Red Sea. Another important project was the fortification of three important cities: Gezer, Megiddo and Hazor. These were all strategically placed, for they were all on the main route that ran through Solomon's kingdom and linked Egypt with Mesopotamia. At Megiddo especially, but perhaps at Hazor and Gezer as well, he built enormous stables. He kept hundreds of horses there. These were chariot horses pulling the armoured war-chariots which enforced Solomon's rule and ensured his control over the trade routes in the Middle East.

Ruins of Solomon's stables at Megiddo, one of the fortified cities (see map).

Debts and other problems

All this cost money. Even though there must have been plenty of money coming into the kingdom from customs tolls, and though Solomon's mines in the desert were extremely profitable, still Solomon had a serious balance of payments deficit. He spent just too much money on luxuries which only benefited the already wealthy aristocracy in Jerusalem. He found himself particularly in debt to Hiram of Tyre, who provided not only sailors for Solomon's ships but also gold, cedar wood and architects for Solomon's buildings. There was only one way to settle his debts with Hiram. Solomon gave him 20 cities in Galilee which had previously been Israelite. It was a bad precedent to set, even though Hiram complained that the cities weren't worth having!

The other way in which Solomon coped with his financial problems was by starting a programme of forced labour. Everybody had to work on the king's building projects for at least one month every year without pay. It seems that it was not only 'vassal people', such as the Edomites, Ammonites and Moabites, who had to do this. It was the Israelites as well—or at least most of them. They didn't like it! People began to remember the warnings which had been given all those years ago when Saul had first become king: 'This is how your king will treat you (. . .) he will make soldiers of your sons; some of them will serve in his war chariots, others in his cavalry, and others will run before his chariots (. . .). He will take your best fields, vineyards and olive groves . . . [I Samuel 8:11–18]. It all seemed to be coming true now!

Local government reorganisation

Read 1 Kings 4:1–19
Solomon was determined. He divided the nation up into 'administrative districts' to make it easier to collect taxes and organise the people for the forced labour projects. Since there were twelve administrative districts, we might imagine that they coincided with the areas which had been settled by the twelve different Israelite tribes. Not so. For Solomon's administrative districts deliberately cut across tribal boundaries. It was a deliberate attempt to weaken the old tribal system. The tribal system

had been essentially democratic, and Solomon felt that it was a threat to his attempt to make himself into an absolute monarch.

There was one significant exception in Solomon's redrawing of the map of the country. The tribe of Judah, Solomon's own tribe, was left intact. It became an administrative district by itself. What is more, most probably the people of Judah did not have to take part in the forced labour programme. They received favoured treatment. That was perhaps Solomon's biggest mistake. Perhaps the Israelite tribes might have been willing to put up with the burden laid upon them as the price for sharing in Solomon's dimly-reflected glory. But to realise that Solomon's own tribe and kinsmen were being treated differently—that was too much. Rebellion was in the air and, as soon as Solomon died and his weaker son Rehoboam had come to the throne, the tribes in the north saw their chance. They were not long in taking it (see *The Progress of God's People* in this series).

Solomon's administrative districts

Mediterranean Sea

Border of Israel
···· District borders
● Fortified cities of Solomon

0   25   50 km

Why are the wicked so successful?

Wise men, such as Solomon himself and the Egyptians he brought to Jerusalem to teach people 'wisdom', believed that a definite order and purpose existed in the world around us. If you could only learn the way the world worked, you could then follow the pattern and you would be successful—which is what 'wisdom' aimed at. There was one basic rule to which the wise men always held—if you did good you would prosper and be successful, but if you did wrong, sooner or later you would meet your downfall. For that, as they saw it, was the way the world worked.

But does the world work like this? That was precisely the question several people asked themselves later in the Hebrew Scriptures. Very often the wicked seemed only too successful, while those who had done good all their lives remained poor and downtrodden. The prophet Jeremiah, who himself suffered a great deal, asked Yahweh explicitly, 'Why are wicked men so prosperous?' **[Jeremiah 12:1]**.

Later on the Book of Job was written to question the presupposition of the wisdom teachers that doing good would inevitably lead to success, and doing evil to disaster. For Job, the good man, suffers disaster after disaster. Finally, after much heart-searching, he comes to the conclusion that true religion is not a matter of rewards and punishments, but of a relationship with Yahweh which will outlast even death.

'Why has all this happened to me?' Job argued with God.

19 The Temple of the Lord

Perhaps Solomon's greatest work, and certainly the one he was most remembered for after his death, when the rest of the splendour of his kingdom had disappeared, was the Temple he built for Yahweh in Jerusalem. You may recall that David had thought of building a temple, but had been discouraged from this. By the time of Solomon, however, society had moved on. The objection made by Nathan—that Yahweh had been a wanderer's god who had always travelled around with his people in a tent—hardly seemed relevant in Solomon's sophisticated and cosmopolitan world.

Cedars of Lebanon

To build his Temple, Solomon called in the experts. That meant once again Hiram, King of Tyre, and workmen from Tyre and the other Phoenician cities such as Sidon and Byblos. The Phoenicians knew all about building, because their country was the land where the cedar tree grew. Cedar trees, growing perhaps to 30 metres tall and immensely strong, provided the long beams necessary for supporting the roof and walls in buildings as large as the Temple.

The Phoenicians were famous throughout the ancient Middle East for their trade in the cedar trees which grew high up on the slopes of Mount Lebanon in Phoenicia. From there cedar was exported for building projects as far as Egypt. The Egyptians sent papyrus and silver to Phoenicia in exchange. From about 1100 BC, a century or so before the time of Solomon, we have an account of a journey made by an Egyptian envoy, Wen-Amon, to the king of Byblos. He had come to buy cedar wood to build the sacred ship of the god Amon-Re. Wen-Amon did not have a pleasant time. He was robbed by the 'Peoples of the Sea' and later on almost murdered in Cyprus. When he got to Byblos the king there deliberately kept him waiting—he wanted to show who was boss! It was only after Wen-Amon had handed over a very large

sum of money that the king of Byblos condescended to begin the lengthy process of chopping down the cedar trees in the mountains and rolling them down to the coast. What a contrast with the courteous way Solomon's envoy was received in Phoenicia a hundred years later!

Over the centuries since the time of Solomon, cedar wood proved so popular that these days there are very few cedar trees left on Mount Lebanon at all. Those that remain are now strictly protected.

Solomon's Temple and Herod's Temple

Where exactly did Solomon build his Temple? Unfortunately, we don't really have any remains of the building. It was destroyed by the Babylonians when they captured Jerusalem in 586 BC. Later on, other temples were built on the same site—first a small one in 520 BC when the people returned from exile in Babylon, and 500 years later a magnificent building was put up by Herod the Great. Herod laid a huge, flat platform for his new Temple building, and this covered everything that had been there before so effectively that it is doubtful if archaeologists could discover anything of Solomon's Temple even if they had the chance.

In Jerusalem today you can still see some traces of Herod's building work. The Temple building itself completely disappeared after its destruction by the Romans in AD 70, but it is easy to see parts of the enormous walls and surface of the platform that Herod erected to support the Temple building. These days, of course, there is a Muslim sanctuary on the site. Though the Muslim 'Dome of the Rock' does not resemble either in shape or appearance the Temples of Solomon or Herod, still its breath-taking beauty and magnificence give us an impression of how travellers to Jerusalem must have felt when they first caught sight of the Temple in the days of its glory. So we do know approximately where the Temple of Solomon was. It was somewhere within the bounds of that huge, flat platform build by Herod. With a bit of detective work, though, we can probably get much closer than that.

The threshing floor of Araunah

Read 2 Samuel 24:18–25
Solomon's Temple was built at the same place as David had previously set up an altar for Yahweh. According to **2 Samuel 24:18–25**, that was on the threshing floor of Araunah the Jebusite. A threshing floor was a place where the newly-harvested grain was threshed and winnowed. It was thrown up into the air with a pitchfork to separate the grain from the outer chaff. There were two requirements for a threshing floor. It had to be a large piece of flat, solid rock, so that the grain would not disappear into crevices. It also had to be high on a hill to catch the wind which helped the process of winnowing. On the site of what was Herod's great Temple platform there is one spot that fulfils both these criteria perfectly. For in the middle of the 'Dome of the Rock' there is a large, flat, solid piece of rock. It is bed-rock, a point where the natural hill breaks through the artificial platform built by Herod. It is the highest point in the area. Almost certainly that rock was the threshing floor of Araunah, and so it was part of Solomon's Temple. Experts disagree as to whether it was used as the base of the altar of sacrifice or whether it provided the foundations for the 'Holy of Holies' of the Temple. All the same, we can be sure that that rock has been a holy place where men have worshipped God, from the time of Araunah the Jebusite through the rest of the Hebrew Scriptures—right down to the present day.

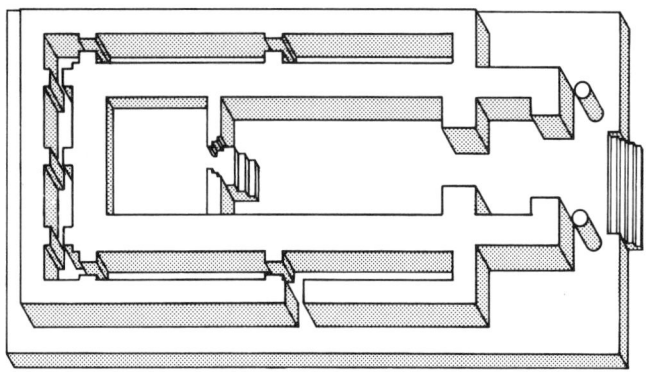

The Temple at Tell Tainat was like Solomon's Temple. It was very close to the king's palace.

What mean these stones?

Read 1 Kings 6–7

What did Solomon's Temple look like? Although we don't have any remains of the Temple itself (except for the Rock), we do find a detailed description of what the Temple looked like in 1 Kings. We can also make use of the Book of Ezekiel, although this was written several centuries later after Solomon's Temple had been destroyed. However, Ezekiel's vision of a new Temple [Ezekiel 40–48] is probably based on what he remembered of the old Temple he had seen in his youth in Jerusalem. In addition, Hiram's Phoenician architects were kind enough to leave us several blueprints and prototypes. For Solomon's Temple was by no means the only one that Phoenician craftsmen built. In present-day Syria and Lebanon, there have been discovered the remains of several temples which could fit in many respects the description of Solomon's Temple given in **1 Kings 6–7**. Particularly close is the temple which was built at Tell Tainat in north Syria in the ninth century BC.

Putting together our impressions of the remains at Tell Tainat and the written details in the Hebrew Scriptures, we can suggest that the Temple built by Solomon had three rooms. There was an inner 'Holy of Holies', a large middle hall and an outer entrance porch. Just outside the building there would have been the altar of sacrifice, on which the priests slaughtered the sacrificial animals on behalf of the people. There was a great deal of rich and elab-

orate decoration in and around the Temple. Within the Holy of Holies, to which only the priests had access, there were two mighty cherubim, sculpted out of olive wood and overlaid with gold. Around the walls of the building there were friezes of palm trees, flowers and cherubim. At the entrance to the Temple stood two mighty pillars, one each side of the doors. They were inscribed with the names Jachin and Boaz. And by the side of the altar stood an enormous bronze bowl. It was filled with water and called the 'Bronze Sea'.

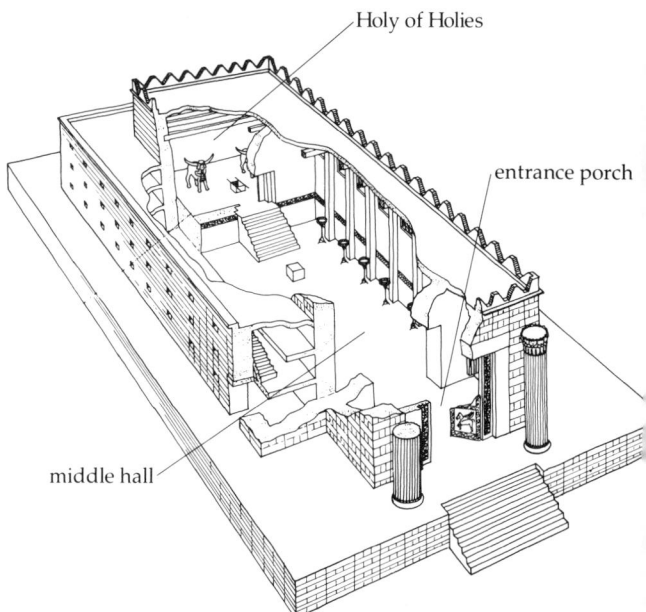

Solomon's three-roomed Temple looked like other temples built by the Phoenicians.

Symbols and meanings

Why all this decoration? What was the purpose of the Bronze Sea? Still today in worship, people make use of symbols. In the Christian Church the candles on the altar symbolise the Light which has come to the world, the water used in baptism symbolises the washing away of sin.

Among religious people, symbols are felt to have a certain power—they bring about that which they symbolise. So it was in Solomon's Temple. Jachin and Boaz represented the strength and security of God, the Bronze Sea symbolised his power over the unruly seas. Inside the Temple building the palm-tree frieze symbolised the life-giving qualities of the Temple, and the cherubim provided a throne for the invisible Yahweh. For what gave the Temple its essential function and meaning was that Yahweh himself dwelt there—Solomon had had the Ark of the Covenant brought to the Holy of Holies and placed above the wings of the gilded cherubim. Now Yahweh dwelt in the Temple, dwelt permanently in Jerusalem. His presence guaranteed the safety of his city. That was Solomon's belief and the belief of many in Jerusalem.

A wanderer's God stood still

Yahweh was tamed and domesticated. He had been put in his house and told to expect visitors! He was to be available as required! But could you do that to Abraham's God, to a wanderer's God who always travelled on ahead of his people? Could you do that to the terrifying God of the Exodus and Sinai, the God who was to be no man's puppet? In the years to come there

Jewish people today have no temple. Instead, they meet for worship in synagogues such as this one.

were to be many questions about the Temple. For all its exquisite beauty, for all the hopes and longings of the pilgrims who wound their way up to Jerusalem, there were many who saw the Temple as a danger to the true worship of Yahweh. Could a God who had always been on the move be made to stand still?

The songs of Yahweh

We have a very good idea of what the worship of Yahweh in Solomon's Temple involved. Many of the psalms in the biblical Book of Psalms were used in the festivals and daily worship offered there. We could even perhaps refer to the Book of Psalms as the 'hymn-book' of the temple. There were psalms for different occasions. In recent years, scholars have been interested in 'classifying' the different kinds we have. Some of the psalms were sung or used by individual Israelites, other psalms were for the whole community of Israel to use together. Many psalms were 'thanksgiving psalms', when people thanked Yahweh for the blessings he had showered upon them (e.g. Psalm 66). Other psalms were 'lamentation psalms' (e.g. Psalm 77). These were used when disaster had struck an individual or the community. 'Lamentation psalms' implored Yahweh to put the situation right, to remove all injustice and oppression. There were also 'Songs of Ascent', psalms sung by pilgrims to Jerusalem as they climbed the steep hills towards the city (e.g. Psalm 122). Yet other psalms were 'royal psalms'. These were particularly concerned with the king, either on his marriage or on his coronation and coming to the throne (e.g. Psalm 45).

Many of the psalms reveal clearly how close a relationship of trust and love there was between the Israelite worshipper and the God whom he worshipped. And so, although the temple in which they were originally sung was destroyed many centuries ago, the psalms themselves have continued to be used again and again by Jewish and Christian people, who are the spiritual heirs of the Israelites who worshipped Yahweh in the great Temple of Solomon.

20 The teller of the tale

The golden age of Israel

In the last few sections we have seen that the time of David and Solomon was in many ways the 'golden age' of Israel. It was a time of great political power and prestige, of elegant buildings, of wealth and luxury shared by at least a few. It was a time when international culture came to Israel—the wisdom of the Egyptians, artistic talents of the Phoenicians. It was a time when the Israelites had the chance to develop the art of writing, a luxury they had not really had the possibility of pursuing before. 'The people of Judah and Israel were as numerous as the grains of sand on the seashore; they ate and drank and were happy. Solomon's kingdom included all the nations from the River Euphrates to Philistia and the Egyptian border.' **[1 Kings 4:20–21]**.

In the kingdom of David and Solomon, there were some people who began to ask questions. They were not necessarily against the changes and developments that the Israelites had experienced in the last few years. In fact they appreciated greatly the leisure for reflection which David's successes had won. All the same, the new glory of the Israelites gave them pause for thought. It had all happened so very quickly. Only a few years before Israel had been a struggling group of tribes, devastated by the war with the Philistines. Now here it was, a great nation, not only free from the dominion of the Philistines, but ruling over an empire which stretched from the Euphrates river as far as the borders of Egypt. Why had it happened like this? What did it mean? And were the people of Israel really up to making use of the new possibilities which had so suddenly come their way?

The Yahwist's answer

One man—or perhaps a group of men—writing most probably in the time of Solomon provided inspired answers to these questions. He wrote down the history of his people to explain why it was that events had happened like this. His history is preserved for us in the Hebrew Scriptures. It is the J writing of the Pentateuch (see section 6). You may remember that the J writer can be distinguished from the other writers of the Pentateuch by the way in which he calls God Yahweh throughout his history, even before the time of Moses. We don't know the name or names of the writer of the J history. Traditionally therefore scholars call him the Yahwist, because he made so great a use of God's special name.

The Yahwist had a number of sources to help him compile his history. Most of these sources were probably *oral*, although a few may already have been written down. Let us look at the

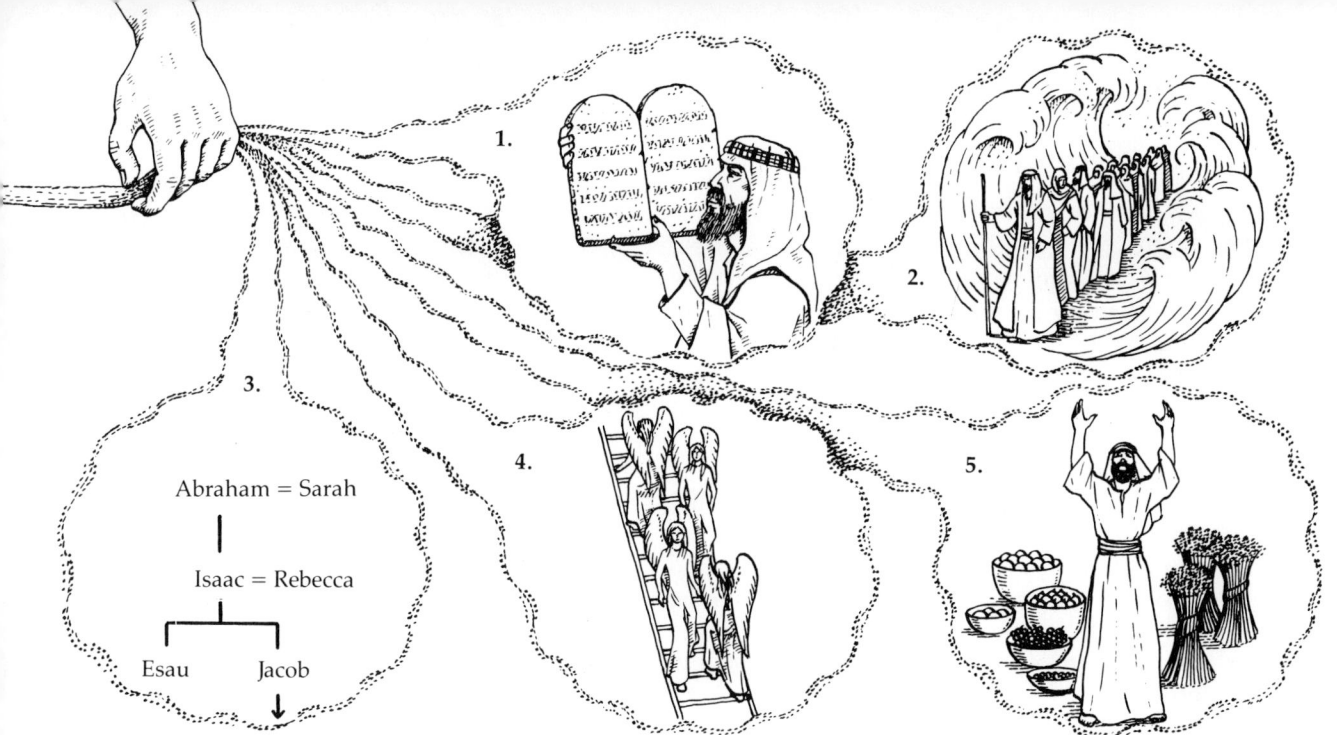

kinds of material the Yahwist made use of in writing his history:

1. Laws
The Yahwist knew the essential laws of his people, such as the Ten Commandments. There were other ancient law codes which had also become important by the time he wrote.

2. Songs
The really great moments in Israel's history, such as crossing the Sea of Reeds, had been celebrated in songs that were remembered from one generation to another.

3. Genealogies
Since family relationships were so very important in tribal society (see section 2), children from a very early age had to learn who their ancestors and kinsfolk were. They were taught by the tribal elders, and they did not need books—they had to have all the details word-perfect inside their heads. One important reason for the Yahwist writing when he did was the weakening of tribal society that happened in the time of David and Solomon. If the names of the ancestors were not written down now, they might soon be forgotten.

4. Tales of the ancestors
Once again, these tales of the adventures of the patriarchs, of Abraham, Isaac and Jacob, which had been handed down for generations in the tribes, had to be written down before they were forgotten.

5. Worship
Whenever they went to pray to God, the people remembered what great things he had done for them and there forefathers. So at the religious festivals of the Israelites, at Passover, Weeks and Ingathering, a great deal of Israelite history was recalled and told. Like other Israelites, the Yahwist would therefore have been familiar with such history.

6. Customs and traditions
Among the Israelites there were several ancient customs and traditions. For example, the Israelites never ate the sinew of the hip of an animal. There was an ancient story which explained the reason for this. It had been in the sinew of the hip that Jacob had been wounded during his fight with God. Other stories explained why particular places had been given appropriate names. The Yahwist knew many such stories and included them in his history.

Writing history, however, is not just a matter of collecting lists of facts from a number of sources. The job of the historian is to arrange these facts in such a way as to give meaning to people's present, past and maybe even future. This the Yahwist has done for us.

The curse and the blessing

Read Genesis 3:1–21, 26

The Yahwist's story began in the very earliest times, the days of Adam and Eve. He told the tale of their original innocence and their life in the Garden of Eden. But then they were deceived by the 'wise' serpent. Yahweh's response was to throw them out of the Garden and put them all under a curse: Adam, Eve, the serpent, the earth, all humankind were roundly cursed by Yahweh. In the next few chapters the word curse appears several times again—first in the story of Cain, then in the story of Noah and the flood. Finally, in the attempt to build the Tower of Babel up to heaven, humankind shows how completely cursed it has become and is scattered across the earth. But then Yahweh himself acts. He resolves to wipe out the curse by offering a blessing in its stead. In **Genesis 12:1–3** we are told of this new beginning. 'The

The Yahwist reflected on humankind: just what are human beings? They are different from other animals, yet they still die like other creatures. The story of the 'forbidden fruit' in the Garden of Eden explains this. People tried to steal 'wisdom' that really only belonged to God. In doing so they lost their innocence, and therefore had to leave Paradise behind.

LORD said to Abram, "Leave your country, your relatives, and your father's home, and go to a land that I am going to show you. I will give you many descendants, and they will become a great nation. I will bless you, and make your name famous, so that you will be a blessing. I will bless those who bless you, but I will curse those who curse you. And through you I will bless all the nations".'

Blessing is the opposite of curse. Five times in those three verses do we read the word 'bless' or 'blessing'. In the stories of the patriarchs that follow, again and again we read of 'blessing'. Abraham is blessed again, and later on Isaac and then Jacob. Read **Genesis 26** and notice how often the idea of blessing appears in this one chapter.

The history of the Yahwist continues through the time the Israelites spent in Egypt. It tells of the Exodus, when blessing was seen in action, and then describes the wandering in the desert. The Yahwist's history seems to end on the borders of Canaan with words which are a prediction of the eventual coming of David and his kingdom.

'A king, like a bright star, will arise in that nation.
Like a comet he will come from Israel!

[Numbers 24:17].

The coming of David was the fulfilment of the blessing which had been promised to Abraham. Now Abraham's descendants had indeed become a great nation—great in name, and great in land. Israel's empire can be explained by the blessing to Abraham.

But is this absolutely all the Yahwist was trying to say? Probably not. He had a warning and a call to give to the Israelites as well.

The warning

The Yahwist did not like all that was going on in Solomon's court. Its sophistication and its self-sufficiency smacked to him of the Tower of Babel. He wasn't even completely sure about that new-fangled wisdom that was making its appearance, coming from Egypt. Remember, it was the 'wise' serpent who had led Adam and Eve astray. Beware Israel!

In the ancient Middle East a story was told of a great flood from which there were few survivors. The Yahwist says the ancient Israelites believed there was a *moral* reason for the flood—humanity was so wicked, a righteous God could no longer tolerate them. This contrasts with the *amoral* view of the story told by the Babylonians, in which humanity is destroyed just because it makes too much noise for the comfort of the gods.

The call

In **Genesis 12:3** the blessing had not stopped at Abraham and his descendants. It was meant to include all the peoples of the earth, 'And through you I will bless all the nations.' As the story had begun with Adam and Eve, the parents of all humankind, and all humankind had been included in the curse, so now it was time for all humankind to be included in the blessing. That was, according to the Yahwist, the reason for Israel's new empire. It gave the descendants of Abraham a chance—if they would take it and use it properly—to bring blessing, justice and peace to all the families of the earth.

It was a visionary call. Did the Israelites hear? Some must have done, for centuries later there came another inspired individual who re-alised that Yahweh had a purpose for all humankind—and Israel was called to be the instrument of this purpose. We cannot do better than close with his words, which form a bridge between the Old Testament and the New:

God created the heavens and stretched them
    out;
    he fashioned the earth and all that lives there;
    he gave life and breath to all its people.
And now the LORD God says to his servant,
'I, the LORD, have called you and given you
    power
    to see that justice is done on earth.
Through you I will make a covenant with all
    peoples;
    through you I will bring light to the nations.
You will open the eyes of the blind
    and set free those who sit in dark prisons.

'I alone am the LORD your God.
    No other god may share my glory;
    I will not let idols share my praise.
The things I predicted have now come true.
Now I will tell you of new things
    even before they begin to happen.'
[Isaiah 42:5–9].

Was cosmopolitan Jerusalem in the time of Solomon a bit like the Tower of Babel? The Yahwist reminds us that it is not our job to make ourselves famous—if we try, it may well prove disastrous. On the other hand, when Abraham fol-lowed God—wherever he led—God promised to make him famous, and did so.

ASSIGNMENTS

An assignment marked with an asterisk relates to material in the boxed portion of the text.

Section 1

1. Think of a modern example of tension or distrust between communities whose ways of life are different. Say how you think a better understanding might be developed between them.
2. Read Psalm 150 and make a list of the different musical instruments mentioned in it. The Israelites learnt from the Canaanites about playing such instruments.
3. The Canaanite farmers used to cultivate olive trees. Find out what you can about olives and list the different ways people made use of them.
4. Read Genesis 11: 1–9. Explain in your own words what this story means.
5. A nomad and a farmer meet at the edge of the desert. Write down the conversation they might have.
6. Why do you think many of the Israelites were tempted to worship Canaanite gods?
7. Find the psalms that mention either Jerusalem or Zion, the name of the mountain on which Jerusalem was built.
* 8. Draw a picture to illustrate the story of Cain and Abel.
* 9. Write the conversation between Cain and Abel which you think might have led to their quarrel.
10. Before David, Israel was really a *religious* community. After David, Israel was a *nation*. Think of ways in which becoming a nation might be dangerous for the faith of the people.
11. The Israelites originally learnt their history by oral tradition. You have probably learnt your own family history in much the same way. Write down what you can remember about who married whom, when, how many children they had, etc.

How far back can you go?
12. *Essay*: What were the major changes in Israelite life that occurred during the time of David?

Section 2

1. How can you explain Abraham's courage in setting out into the unknown as he did? (Hebrews 11: 8–10 in the New Testament may help you to answer this question.)
2. Imagine you are a child living with your rich family in a fine house in Mari. Describe what your parents have told you about the Amorites.
3. How has archaeology helped us to understand the way Abraham's family lived?
4. Think of ways in which the history of your own country has been affected by its geography and climate.
5. Read Genesis 16: 1–16 carefully. Imagine you are Hagar. Describe your feelings when Sarah drives you away. Say what happens next.
* 6. Choose any sentence from section 2 and work out how many symbols would be needed to write it in Mesopotamian cuneiform.
7. Imagine you are a Beduin family. Describe a typical day in your life.
8. Draw a picture of an 'extended' Beduin family near their tent.
9. Imagine a Beduin family gathered around the fire in the evening. What do you think they might talk about? What kind of stories might they tell?
10. What do you think would be the most important thing a Beduin father would teach his children about God?
11. Write an imaginary 'log-book' that Abraham might have kept as he journeyed from Ur round to Canaan.
12. *Essay*: What do we know about Abraham and his journey from Ur to Canaan?

Section 3

1. What distinctive ideas of God might the following people have: a farmer, a sailor, a doctor, a mother? Make up a short prayer that each of them might use.

2. What difference does it make if you believe God 'stays in one place' or is 'on the move'?

3. Draw a picture of Abraham about to sacrifice Isaac, his son.

4. What 'sacrifices', if any, do you think we are required to make today?

* 5. Later in Israelite history some of the prophets attacked the whole system of sacrifices. Why do you think they felt sacrifice was so dangerous?

6. Imagine you are Abraham. Tell the story of how God made a covenant with you.

7. A covenant involves a binding promise. What other examples of covenants can you find in (a) the Bible, (b) modern life?

8. Read Genesis 24. Describe Rebecca's feelings as she leaves her parents for the journey to Canaan to marry Isaac.

9. Read Genesis 27. Tell the story of Jacob and Esau in your own words.

10. Look at the picture of Jacob's dream on p. 17. What did Jacob learn from his dream? (See Genesis 28: 13–15). Do you think God still speaks to us in dreams?

11. Imagine you are Jacob. Write an account of your reunion with your brother. Be sure to say what happened to you the night before the meeting.

12. *Essay*: Why can we describe Abraham and the other patriarchs as 'men of faith'?

Section 4

1. Draw a series of simple pictures to tell the story recorded in Genesis 37.

2. On a casette, record an 'interview' with Joseph's brothers. Pretend you are a reporter trying to get at the truth of what happened to Joseph.

3. Read Genesis 39–40. Imagine you are Joseph, in prison, falsely accused of attacking Potiphar's wife. Make up a prayer to God about your situation.

4. The brothers went down to Egypt because of a famine. Famines still happen today. Find out in which areas of the world they are most common. Use reference material to help you.

5. Imagine you are an Egyptian border official. You have allowed several groups of hungry nomads into Egypt. Write a letter to Pharaoh explaining why.

6. Copy the picture of the scribe on p. 20. Decorate the edges with hieroglyphs.

7. Read the story of how Joseph was found and reunited with his brothers and father. Draw a series of pictures to illustrate it.

8. Imagine you are a nomad who visits the court of Pharaoh. Write down your impressions.

9. The stories of Joseph give us a taste of the bureaucracy of ancient Egypt. Look through the stories and list all the different officials mentioned in them.

10. Look through the Book of Proverbs. Compile your own anthology of sayings which strike you as still being wise today.

11. Imagine you are a 'junior scribe' in Egypt, helping Joseph with his famine relief programme. Write a letter to your brother, a farmer, explaining your job and how important it is.

12. *Essay*: 'You plotted evil against me, but God turned it into good' (Genesis 50:20). How does the story of Joseph and his brothers illustrate this?

Section 5

1. From earliest times, people have worshipped the sun as a god. Why do you think they have done this?

* 2. Imagine you are a supporter of the reform of Akhenaton. Explain why you prefer his ideas to the traditional polytheistic beliefs of Egypt. (Look back to section 4.)

3. Many religions, even today, are polytheistic, although both Judaism and Christianity are not. Find some reasons why polytheistic ideas are still attractive to many people.

4. Make up an imaginary letter from a Hebrew slave to his family still in Canaan.

5. Look through the first few chapters of Exodus. How many times does the word 'Hebrew' or 'Hebrews' appear? Does it seem to describe people of low status?

6. The Egyptians treated the Israelites so badly partly because they were immigrants. Do people still treat immigrants badly? How could this be made better?

7. In the nineteenth century, black slaves in America sang 'spirituals' comparing their slavery to that of the Israelites in Egypt. Find examples of spirituals, and learn one.
8. Draw a picture of an Egyptian Pharaoh from about 1300 BC.
9. Imagine you are Pharaoh explaining to your wife why you decided to kill the Israelite baby boys. Write the dialogue between you.
10. People often like to tell exciting stories about great men. Find out about a great personage in your country's history who came from a very 'lowly' background.
11. Imagine you are the Egyptian princess who found the infant Moses. Tell the story of what happened.
12. *Essay*: What is meant by calling the Israelites 'Hebrew slaves' in Egypt?

Section 6

1. At the 'burning bush', Moses met God. Draw a picture of this experience.
2. Moses takes off his shoes, because he is on 'holy ground'. In many religions this is still the custom. Find some examples.
3. Read Isaiah 6:1–8. What does this experience suggest about God's holiness?
4. What does 'holy' mean to *you*? If someone was described as a holy person, what would you expect him or her to be like?
5. Read Exodus 19: 16–19. Paint a picture to express something of the majesty of Mount Sinai (see p. 27).
6. Imagine you are Moses telling Jethro what happened at the burning bush. What would you say?
* 7. Do you think names are still important? Do you know what your own name means? Do *you* like your own name?
8. What story have we read so far of someone's name being changed? Does the change have an important meaning?
9. Give examples from the Bible when something important happens on a mountain.
10. Read Exodus 1–3. Draw a sequence of small pictures to illustrate the story.
11. The story in Exodus 1–3 shows that God cares when he sees people suffer. Say how religious people try to witness to this.

12. *Essay*: Why is the story of God revealing his name to Moses so important?

Section 7

1. Write a short 'front page' story about the ten plagues for an Egyptian newspaper.
2. Read Exodus 7: 8–13. Write a short play about the dramatic confrontation between Moses and Pharaoh in that chapter.
3. Find out which areas of the world are still affected by plagues of locusts. What can be done to control the locusts?
4. Use an atlas to make a tracing of the Nile. How do people today control its floods?
5. Do you think miracles still happen? List arguments *for* or *against* this idea.
6. Imagine you are a member of an Israelite family. Describe the exciting events of Passover night from your point of view.
7. Find out how the Jewish Passover is celebrated today. (Use reference material.)
8. The Passover was originally a nomadic festival. What changes did nomads expect to meet on their journey in the spring?
9. Draw a picture of one of the ten plagues.
10. Read John 1:29–34. What title is given to Jesus that links him to the Passover story?
11. Explain in your own words why the Jewish festival is called 'Passover'.
12. *Essay:* What does the story of the ten plagues tell us about the way God works?

Section 8

1. Copy out and decorate with pictures some of the verses you like from the 'Song of Moses' (Exodus 15: 1–18).
2. Imagine you are an Egyptian officer. Give Pharaoh *your* account of what happened at the 'Sea of Reeds'.
3. Draw a picture of the Israelites crossing the 'Sea of Reeds'.
4. Compare Psalms 96 and 98 with Exodus 15: 1–18. List the points of similarity.
5. Do you think it still makes sense to speak of God 'fighting'?
6. Imagine you are Moses. The Israelites are complaining to you just before the 'Sea of Reeds'. Make up your speech of reply.
7. 'Let my people go!' said God. What

groups of people are there today about whom God might say the same?

8. Explain why the sea the Israelites crossed was probably *not* the Red Sea.

9. Do you think the Israelites spent exactly forty years in the wilderness?

10. The 'Song of Moses' refers to other enemies of Israel. What are they? Where did they live?

*11. Design a colourful banner about the 'New Exodus'. Isaiah 35 will help.

12. *Essay*: Why could we describe the Exodus as *the* most important event in Israelite history?

Section 9

1. In what ways can hard conditions and difficult times be a 'test of faith' for people today? Give an example.

2. Write an imaginary letter from one of the Israelites to Moses, listing your complaints about the situation in the desert.

3. Draw a picture of Moses being given the Ten Commandments on Mount Sinai.

4. Which of the Ten Commandments do you think are (a) the most important to obey, (b) the hardest to obey? Why?

5. Is the second commandment really out of date, or do people still make for themselves 'images' and 'idols' of a kind?

6. 'Do not commit murder.' How relevant do you think this is to (a) abortion, (b) euthanasia, (c) capital punishment?

7. Do you think the commandment about the Sabbath day has anything to say about how Christians spend Sunday?

8. 'Respect your father and your mother.' Give examples of how this can be obeyed when we are (a) children, (b) adults.

9. 'Do not commit adultery.' Find out and explain precisely what this means.

10. 'Do not steal.' This commandment applies to groups as well as individuals. Give examples of ways in which nations steal.

11. Read Exodus 32. Imagine and describe the scene when Moses finds people worshipping the golden calf.

12. *Essay*: Why can Exodus 19: 3–5 be described as the 'heart of the Hebrew Scriptures' message'?

Section 10

1. Imagine you are the King of Edom. Say why you have refused to allow the Israelites to pass through your land. Remember that your ancestor was Esau, Jacob's brother!

2. Read Joshua 4: 19–24. What is the crossing of the Jordan compared to?

3. Read Joshua 1: 1–9. What are the promises, warnings and commands that God gives Joshua?

4. Read Joshua 5: 13–15. Who do you think was the stranger who appeared to Joshua, and what was the meaning and purpose of the meeting?

5. Imagine you are a soldier who fought in the battle of Jericho. Write your diary for that day.

6. Do you think God really wanted all the inhabitants of Jericho to be killed, or is this a wrong understanding of what God is like?

7. Read Joshua 9 and see how the Gibeonites come to terms with Joshua. Draw a picture to illustrate the story.

8. Compare Joshua 10: 28–43 with Judges 1. List any differences. Which version do you think is more accurate?

9. Look up Genesis 49: 14–15. What does this tell us about the tribe of Issachar?

10. At Shechem the Israelites renewed their promise to 'serve the Lord'. What would it mean if someone did this today?

*11. The 'Book of the Covenant' insists that the poor be treated justly and fairly. Find examples of this.

12. *Essay*: Was the entry of the Israelites into Canaan a 'conquest' or a 'settlement'? Give reasons for your answer.

Section 11

1. An Israelite tribesman meets a Canaanite farmer. They discuss their religious beliefs. Write down their conversation.

2. Design a poster for the 'Region of Canaan'.

3. The Israelites believed in one God, the Canaanites in many gods. How did this affect the way people prayed?

4. Imagine you are an Israelite farmer who

believes in Yahweh, but your neighbour, whose crops have failed, is strongly tempted to worship Baal. What arguments would you use to discourage him?

5. Read 1 Kings 18 and draw a picture to illustrate Elijah's conflict with the prophets of Baal.

6. Find out when exactly the Jewish New Year will be celebrated this year.

* 7. Draw a series of small pictures to illustrate the different 'times' listed in the Gezer Calendar.

8. Using Deuteronomy 26: 1–11, write a play about what happened when a 'thank-offering' was brought to the temple.

9. Do religions other than the Jewish faith still celebrate harvest? How?

10. The Feast of Ingathering or Tabernacles is still a very important Jewish feast. Find out how it is celebrated today.

11. Read the instructions in Leviticus 23: 33–44 for celebrating the Feast of Tabernacles. Why is it celebrated?

12. *Essay*: How did the Israelites turn *harvest* festivals into *historical* festivals?

Section 12

1. Using Genesis 49 and Deuteronomy 33, design a sequence of twelve symbols representing each of the twelve tribes.

2. Read Genesis 49. The writer believes that a 'king' will be born from one of the tribes. Which one?

3. Look at Deuteronomy 33: 8–11. What does it tell you about the job of a priest in ancient Israel?

4. Tell the story of the defeat of Jabin and the death of Sisera in a sequence of small pictures.

5. Prepare a dramatic reading (for several voices) of the Song of Deborah.

6. Which Israelite tribes are not mentioned in the Song of Deborah?

7. Read Judges 6 and say in your own words how Gideon was called to rescue Israel.

8. Imagine you are a Midianite soldier who escaped after the defeat of your army by Gideon. Give your account of what happened.

9. Imagine you are Gideon and people are

offering you the kingship. Write your speech of refusal.

10. What do you think is the moral of the strange story of the trees which decided to choose a king? (Judges 9: 7–15)

11. Imagine you are an Israelite 'judge'. Give a list of the problems you face.

12. *Essay*: What are the main lessons the writer of the story of Gideon wanted us to learn from it?

Section 13

1. Imagine you are a Philistine, proud of your heritage. Give a brief account of your history as a people.

2. Paint a picture of a major volcanic eruption, such as that of Santorini.

3. Write a dialogue between an Israelite and a Philistine about the Israelite asking to be taught how to work iron.

4. Read the Samson stories (Judges 13–16). What would you say we are supposed to learn from them?

5. Write a 'newspaper report' of the events that led up to death Samson's (Judges 16).

7. Draw a map of the coastline of Palestine (see p. 55) and mark on it the five Philistine cities.

* 8. Read Psalm 107: 23–32. Compose a prayer that sailors might use in a storm at sea.

9. Draw a picture of a Phoenician ship.

*10. Read Jonah 1: 1–2:10 and Acts 27. What do these stories tell us about people's attitudes to the sea?

11. Read Mark 4:35–41. What is the story really saying about Jesus?

12. *Essay*: Who were the Philistines and why did they affect the Israelites to such an extent?

Section 14

1. 'Everyone did just as he pleased.' Consider and describe what would happen if every member of (a) your family, (b) your school, (c) your country was allowed to do just as he or she liked.

2. Read again the story of Samuel. Imagine you are Samuel as an old man. How would you describe your experience now?

3. Samuel was only a child, yet God called

him. Find and describe an incident in the Gospels where children are shown to be important to Jesus too.

4. Do you think parents today should take young children to church?

5. Find out about *one* person in the twentieth century who might deserve the title of prophet.

6. Draw a picture of Israelite prophets.

7. Imagine you are an Israelite mother and your son wants to become a prophet. Write a speech trying to discourage him. 1 Samuel 10: 5–13 and 19:18–24 may help.

8. Write a short comedy about the havoc the Ark of the Covenant caused in the Philistine territory.

* 9. Make up a short story which illustrates the effect that 'words' can have even today.

*10. Read the opening verses of John's gospel. Why do you think Jesus is described here as the 'Word'?

11. Read Jeremiah 28. Why was Jeremiah unpopular with his fellow countrymen?

12. *Essay*: Why did the Israelites want a king?

Section 15

1. Draw a picture of Samuel anointing Saul.
2. Who else in earlier Israelite history broke the traditions of 'holy war', as Saul did?
3. Do you think kings and queens today are 'above the law'? Should they be?
4. Read 1 Samuel 15: 1–35. Describe the battle with the Amalekites and its outcome from Saul's point of view.
5. Have you ever felt that God has rejected you or is angry with you? Why was this? How did you cope with it?
6. Read 1 Samuel 16: 1–13. Produce a short 'radio report' on the anointing of David, recording interviews with Samuel, Jesse, David and one or two of his brothers.
7. Read 1 Samuel 17. Imagine you are a war correspondent reporting on the Philistine–Israeli conflict. File your story on the encounter between David and Goliath.
8. Record a short 'interview' with David after he defeats Goliath. Get David to explain how someone as young as he was defeated the Philistine champion.
9. Read 1 Samuel 24. Imagine you are one of David's men. Describe how your master spared Saul and say what your feelings are about this.

10. Read 1 Samuel 28. Witchcraft is forbidden in the Bible. What do you think of people's interest in the supernatural today?

*11. Prepare a dramatic reading of David's famous lament over Jonathan and Saul (2 Samuel 1: 19–27).

12. *Essay*: Why was Saul a failure?

Section 16

1. Imagine you are a woman of Jerusalem. David is besieging your city. Do you feel secure or not? Describe your feelings.

2. Imagine you are one of David's soldiers. Describe how you captured Jerusalem.

3. Draw a picture of an ancient siege.

4. Imagine you are David's wife, Michal. Write a letter to your sister describing David's behaviour when the Ark was brought to Jerusalem.

4. Do you think dancing has a place in the worship of God? Suggests ways in which religious services might be made more joyful.

5. It is said of one of David's sons, 'His father had never reprimanded him about anything' (1 Kings 1:6). How did David suffer the consequences of having 'spoilt' his children?

6. Read 2 Samuel 8 and 10. Make a list of all the peoples whom David captured.

7. Fresh water was very precious in Canaan. We could call it the 'water of life'. How does this help us understand John 4: 1–15?

8. Imagine you are David. After a long wait, you have just heard that Absalom is dead. Write your diary for that night.

9. If you were Joab, how would you justify to David the fact that you killed Absalom? Read 2 Samuel 18: 1–33.

*10. Jerusalem's beauty has led to its sorrow. Give examples of other things or places that people fight over because they feel so deeply about them.

11. Read Revelations 21–22:5. Draw a picture of the 'new Jerusalem' based on this.

12. *Essay*: Explain what David achieved by making Jerusalem his capital.

Section 17

1. Suppose that one of the first Hebrew nomads could travel through time to David's reign. What would he find surprising about Israel then?
2. You are a 'conservative' Israelite who does not like some of David's ideas. Present a list of your objections to him.
3. Read Psalm 72 carefully. What does it say the Israelites expect from their king?
4. David took a census of his people. Censuses are regularly taken today. Do you think they are a good or a bad idea? Why?
5. There was probably some tension between the 'Sinai covenant' and the 'Davidic covenant'. Why?
6. In the time of David, Israel became a nation. What do people need to be a nation?
7. Read 2 Samuel 7: 1–17. Why doesn't Yahweh need a house?
8. How many of the Ten Commandments did David break in his dealings with Uriah and Bathsheba?
9. 'You are the man.' Write a short play of Nathan confronting King David.
10. The story of Elijah and Ahab (1 Kings 21) is similar to the story of Nathan and David (1 Samuel 12). List the points of similarity.
*11. Read Matthew 21:1–11. Were people right to call Jesus 'Son of David'?
12. *Essay*: In the light of the stories we have studied about him, write a short character assessment of David.

Section 18

1. Design a poster to illustrate different aspects of 'Solomon in all his glory'.
2. Sheba or Yemen is sometimes called the 'frankincense land'. Find out about frankincense and its use.
3. What kinds of officials did Solomon's bureaucracy include?
4. In 1 Kings 4:33, the 'Lebanon cedars' (see picture on p. 78) are contrasted with 'the hyssop that grows on walls'. What is the point of the contrast?
5. Read 1 Kings 3: 16–28. Imagine you are one of the mothers, and tell your version of the story.

6. What did Solomon think about how *children* should behave? (See Proverbs 13: 1, 24; 15:5; 17:21, 25; 23:13, 14; 29: 15, 17; 30: 17.) Would you agree with him?
7. If Solomon wrote Proverbs 31:10–31, do you agree with his view of marriage?
8. Imagine you are a member of the tribe of Issachar. Do you like the way you are being treated by Solomon? How would you prefer him to treat you?
9. Make a list of the kind of people who probably appreciated Solomon's reign.
10. Read Ecclesiastics 1–3. What is the author's attitude to life?
*11. Are wicked people more prosperous than those who do good? If so, what is the reason for doing good?
12. *Essay*: Was Solomon a wise king?

Section 19

1. Imagine you are a visitor to Jerusalem at the time of Solomon. Describe what impression his temple makes on you.
2. Read 1 Kings 6: 15–38. Make a series of drawings to illustrate the interior furnishings of the temple.
3. The temple was rich in *symbols*. What symbols are used today in Christian churches and services of worship?
4. Do we need special buildings in order to worship God? How are church buildings useful or helpful?
5. When Yahweh dwelt in his temple in Jerusalem, many Israelites believed this guaranteed the safety of the city. Why?
6. Read Jeremiah 7: 1–15. What did this prophet think about the temple acting as a 'guarantee'?
7. According to the Revelation of John 21:22, in the new Jerusalem there will be no 'temple in the city, because its temple is the Lord God Almighty and the Lamb'. Why is a temple not necessary in the new Jerusalem?
8. Imagine you are an Israelite from a village, setting off on a pilgrimage to Jerusalem and the temple. Describe your feelings. Psalms 84 and 122 will help you.
* 9. Write out a few of the Psalms you like, taking care to include different types.

*10. Choose one Psalm. Copy it out and 'illuminate' it as beautifully as you can.
*11. Read Psalm 23. Why do you think it has meant so much to people for almost 3000 years?
 12. *Essay*: If you were a thoughtful person and knew something of Israel's history, what might worry you about Solomon's temple and the worship there?

Section 20

1. Read Genesis 2:5–25. Use this chapter to paint a picture of the Garden of Eden.
2. What similarities do you notice between the description of 'Eden' in Genesis 2 and the picture of the 'new Jerusalem' in Revelation 21? Are they significant?
3. Read Genesis 3. Who do you think was most to blame for the disaster?
4. The name 'Adam' means 'man'. Do you think the story of Adam and Eve can be viewed as an example of an illuminating experience all people go through?
5. In what sense do you think the story of Adam and Eve is a 'true' story?
6. Genesis 22:25–31 and 32: 22–32 are 'explanation' stories. What do they explain?
7. How many times does the word 'bless' or 'blessing' appear in Genesis 26?
8. Study the two lists of blessings in Deuteronomy 28: 1–16 and Matthew 5: 1–11. How do they differ?
9. Why is there more to the story of Israel than the history of one little nation?
10. Does the Yahwist have a call for us today?
11. What does it mean to say Israel is a 'light to the nations'?
12. *Essay*: What did the Yahwist do and why do you think his work was so important?

The Hebrews and Palestine to the end of Solomon's reign

Date BC	The Israelites	Other people in the Middle East
2000		End of the Sumerians
		The Amorite invasion
1800	Abraham	
	Isaac	The Hyksos invade Egypt
	Jacob and Esau	
1700	Jacob's family goes to Egypt	
1600–1500	The Israelites become slaves	End of Hyksos rule in Egypt
c. 1285	The Exodus	Pharaoh Rameses II
c. 1220	The Israelites settle in Canaan	The Merneptah pillar
c. 1150	Period of the 'judges'	The Philistines settle in Canaan
c. 1050	Shiloh destroyed; the Ark captured	
1020–1000	Samuel and Saul	
1000–961	Reign of David	
961–922	Solomon is king	
922	When Solomon dies, the kingdom is divided	

Index

This index is selective and designed to help the student find the most important information about key topics. References in **bold** type denote boxes, and those in *italics* refer to pictures or their captions.